MathFlare

Name: _______________________

Class: ___________

Teacher: _______________________

Introduction

As parents and educators, we recognize the pivotal role mathematics plays in shaping a child's academic journey and future success. Yet, the path to mathematical proficiency can often seem daunting, fraught with challenges and complexities. That's where the transformative power of MathFlare Workbooks shine through, illuminating the way forward with clarity, precision, and purpose.

Introducing MathFlare Workbooks – a beacon of guidance, a testament to excellence, and a catalyst for achievement. Crafted with meticulous care and expertise, MathFlare Workbooks stand as paragons of educational excellence, designed to nurture young minds, ignite a passion for learning, and develop a deep-rooted understanding of mathematical concepts.

Picture this: your child eagerly delves into the pages of Mathflare Workbook, greeted by a step-by-step guide illuminated with vivid examples that demystify complex mathematical concepts. With each turn of the page, they embark on a journey of discovery, encountering thoughtfully curated practice questions that reinforce learning and hone problem-solving skills. And when they unveil the answers to those very questions, a sense of accomplishment blossoms within them – a tangible reward for their hard work and dedication.

But MathFlare Workbooks are more than just tools for learning; they are pathways to comprehension, fostering a deep-seated understanding of mathematical concepts through a sequential, logical flow. From fundamental principles to advanced problem-solving strategies, every chapter builds upon the last, ensuring a robust foundation upon which future knowledge can be constructed.

As parents, we yearn for nothing more than to see our children thrive, to witness the spark of inspiration ignited within them as they conquer academic challenges with confidence and poise. MathFlare Workbooks serve as partners in this noble endeavor, offering not just practice questions, but the keys to unlocking a world of opportunity.

And for teachers, MathFlare Workbooks stand as invaluable allies in the quest to cultivate mathematical proficiency in the classroom. With answers readily available, instructors can focus on guiding and nurturing their students, confident in the knowledge that MathFlare Workbooks provide a solid framework upon which to build.

In the pages of MathFlare Workbooks, we find not just the promise of academic excellence, but the seeds of a brighter tomorrow. So let us embrace the power of mathematics, let us champion the journey of learning, and let us pave the way for a generation of young minds poised to shape the world. With MathFlare Workbooks as our guide, the possibilities are infinite, and the future, bright.

Table of Contents

MathFlare
Grade 2
MATH WORKBOOK
Step by Step Guide and Essential Practice with Answers
Addition
Subtraction
Multiplication
Place Value and Expanded Notations
Geometry
MathFlare Publishing

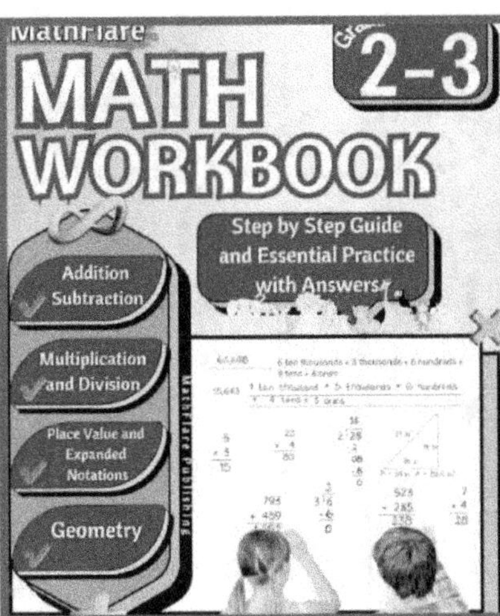
MathFlare
Grade 2-3
MATH WORKBOOK
Step by Step Guide and Essential Practice with Answers
Addition
Subtraction
Multiplication and Division
Place Value and Expanded Notations
Geometry
MathFlare Publishing

MathFlare
Grade 3
MATH WORKBOOK
Step by Step Guide and Essential Practice with Answers
Multiplication and Division
Decimals
Place Value and Expanded Notations
Fractions and Geometry
MathFlare Publishing

MathFlare
Grade 1
MATH WORKBOOK
Step by Step Guide and Essential Practice with Answers
Counting and Numbers
Addition and Subtraction
Place Value and Expanded Notations
Understanding Time
MathFlare Publishing

MathFlare
Grade 1-2
MATH WORKBOOK
Step by Step Guide and Essential Practice with Answers
Counting and Numbers
Addition and Subtraction
Place Value and Expanded Notations
Understanding Time
MathFlare Publishing

MathFlare
Grade 3-4
MATH WORKBOOK
Step by Step Guide and Essential Practice with Answers
Addition Subtraction
Multiplication Division
Place Value and Expanded Notations
Fractions and Geometry
MathFlare Publishing

MathFlare
Grade 4
MATH WORKBOOK
Step by Step Guide and Essential Practice with Answers
Addition Subtraction
Multiplication Division
Place Value and Expanded Notations
Fractions and Geometry
MathFlare Publishing

MathFlare
Grade 4-5
MATH WORKBOOK
Step by Step Guide and Essential Practice with Answers
Multiplication Division
Place Value and Expanded Notations
Fractions and Geometry
Unit Conversion
MathFlare Publishing

MathFlare
MATH WORKBOOK
Grade 5
Step by Step Guide and Essential Practice with Answers
Multiplication Division
Place Value and Expanded Notations
Fractions and Geometry
Unit Conversion
MathFlare Publishing

MathFlare
MATH WORKBOOK
Grade 5-6
Step by Step Guide and Essential Practice with Answers
Multiplication Division
Place Value and Expanded Notations
Fractions and Geometry
Units and Statistics
MathFlare Publishing

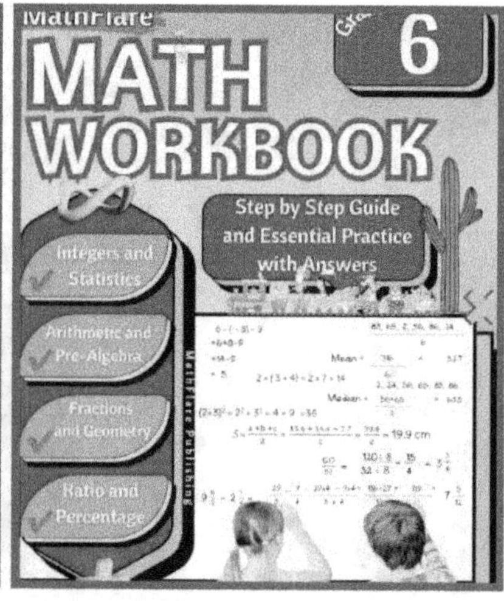
MathFlare
MATH WORKBOOK
Grade 6
Step by Step Guide and Essential Practice with Answers
Integers and Statistics
Arithmetic and Pre-Algebra
Fractions and Geometry
Ratio and Percentage
MathFlare Publishing

MathFlare
MATH WORKBOOK
Grade 6-7
Step by Step Guide and Essential Practice with Answers
Arithmetic and Pre-Algebra
Ratio, Percent Proportion
Geometry
Statistics
MathFlare Publishing

MathFlare
MATH WORKBOOK
Grade 7
Step by Step Guide and Essential Practice with Answers
Pre-Algebra
Ratio, Percent Proportion
Geometry
Statistics
MathFlare Publishing

MathFlare
MATH WORKBOOK
Grade 7-8
Step by Step Guide and Essential Practice with Answers
Pre-Algebra
Ratio, Percent Proportion
Geometry and Cartesian Plane
Statistics
MathFlare Publishing

MathFlare
MATH WORKBOOK
Grade 8-9
Step by Step Guide and Essential Practice with Answers
Pre-Algebra
Ratio, Proportion and Percentage
Linear Equations
Geometry and Cartesian Plane
MathFlare Publishing

MathFlare
MATH WORKBOOK
Grade 8
Step by Step Guide and Essential Practice with Answers
Pre-Algebra
Percentage
Linear Equations
Geometry
MathFlare Publishing

Place Value and Expanded Notations

Place value tells us the value of a digit in a number based on where it's placed.

Imagine we have the number 5,987,647.52843. It has 12 digits.

Now, each digit holds a special place. Let's break down the number 5,987,647.52843:

- The digit 5 is in the millions place. Its value is 5 × 1,000,000=5,000,000.

- The digit 9 is in the hundred thousands place. Its value is 9×100,000=900,000.

- The digit 8 is in the ten thousands place. Its value is 8×10,000=80,000.

- The digit 7 is in the thousands place. Its value is 7×1,000=7,000.

- The digit 6 is in the hundreds place. Its value is 6×100=600.

- The digit 4 is in the tens place. Its value is 4×10=40.

- The digit 7 is in the ones place. Its value is 7×1=7.

- The digit 5 is in the tenths place. Its value is $5 \times \frac{1}{10} = 0.5$.

- The digit 2 is in the hundredths place. Its value is $2 \times \frac{1}{100} = 0.02$.

- The digit 8 is in the thousandths place. Its value is $8 \times \frac{1}{1000} = 0.008$.

- The digit 4 is in the ten thousandths place. Its value is $4 \times \frac{1}{10,000} = 0.0004$.

- The digit 3 is in the hundred thousandths place. Its value is $3 \times \dfrac{1}{100,000} =$ 0.00003.

When we add these values together, we find the value of the entire number:

$$5,000,000 + 900,000 + 80,000 + 7,000 + 600 + 40 + 7 + 0.5 + 0.02 + 0.008$$
$$+ 0.0004 + 0.00003 = 5,987,647.52843$$

Let's solve some problems:

Place value of the underlined digit:

$$9,216.4679\underline{5} = \underline{5 \text{ hundred thousandths}}$$

Expanded notations:

442,218.932 — 4 hundred thousands + 4 ten thousands + 2 thousands + 2 hundreds + 1 ten + 8 ones + 9 tenths + 3 hundredths + 2 thousandths

81,315,897.3 — 80,000,000 + 1,000,000 + 300,000 + 10,000 + 5,000 + 800 + 90 + 7 + 0.3

50,131,193.9 — 5 ten millions + 1 hundred thousand + 3 ten thousands + 1 thousand + 1 hundred + 9 tens + 3 ones + 9 tenths

Rounding Numbers

Rounding numbers is the process of approximating a numerical value to a certain degree of accuracy by replacing it with a simpler or more convenient value. Rounding is commonly used to simplify calculations and express numbers in a more manageable form.

Steps to Rounding Numbers:

1. **Identify the digit to be rounded:** Determine the digit to which the number will be rounded.

2. **Look at the next digit:** Examine the digit immediately to the right of the one being rounded.

3. **Decide whether to round up or down:** If the next digit is 5 or greater, round the digit up. If it is less than 5, round the digit down.

4. **Adjust the number:** Change the digit being rounded and replace all digits to the right with zeros if necessary.

Properties of Rounding Numbers:
1. **Accuracy:** Rounding reduces the precision of a number but maintains its approximate value.

2. **Simplicity:** Rounding simplifies calculations by using fewer digits.

3. **Ease of Use:** Rounding makes numbers easier to work with, especially in mental arithmetic and estimation.

Methods of Rounding Numbers:

1. **Round to Nearest Integer:** Round to the nearest whole number.

    I.   Round Up (Ceiling): Always round up to the nearest integer.

    II. Round Down (Floor): Always round down to the nearest integer.

2. **Round to Nearest Tenth:** Round to the nearest tenth (one decimal place).

3. **Round to Nearest Hundredth:** Round to the nearest hundredth (two decimal places).

4. **Round to Nearest Thousandth:** Round to the nearest thousandth (three decimal places).

5. **Round to Specific Decimal Places:** Round to a specified number of decimal places as needed.

Let's round the number **438,576.214** to various degrees of accuracy:

Rounding Level	Rounded Number	Difference from Original
Nearest Whole Number	438,576	0
Nearest Ten	438,580	+4
Nearest Hundred	438,600	+24
Nearest Thousand	439,000	+424
Nearest Ten Thousand	440,000	+3,424
Nearest Hundred Thousand	400,000	−38,576
Nearest Million	0.4386×10^6	−438,576.214

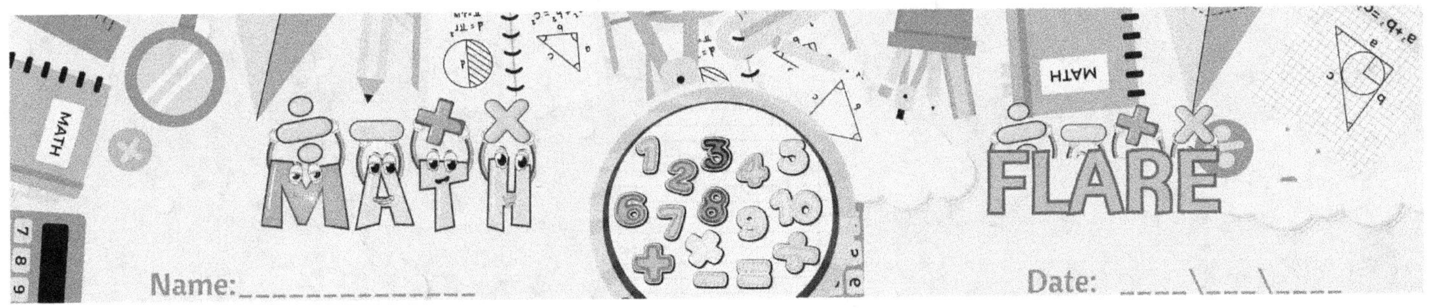

Place Value

Determine the place value of the underlined digit.

1. 7,083,492.788 = _______________________________________

2. 4,962,182.628 = _______________________________________

3. 6,819,163.772 = _______________________________________

4. 7,234,687.322 = _______________________________________

5. 9,738,650.468 = _______________________________________

6. 3,984,400.941 = _______________________________________

7. 6,284,423.78 = _______________________________________

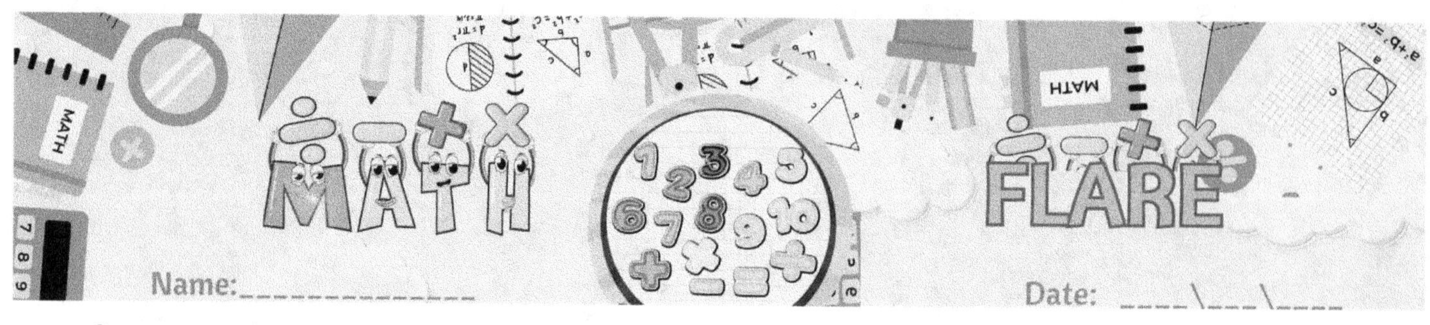

8. 7,451,399.<u>7</u>39 = _______________________________

9. 1,296,150.79<u>4</u> = _______________________________

10. 8,123,539.0<u>8</u>2 = _______________________________

11. 4,454,6<u>4</u>9.795 = _______________________________

12. 8,<u>8</u>13,947.867 = _______________________________

13. 6,234,197.6<u>0</u>1 = _______________________________

14. <u>4</u>,872,971.576 = _______________________________

15. 1,907,390.<u>6</u>06 = _______________________________

16. 3,510,190.2̲97 = _______________________________

17. 9,006,136̲.827 = _______________________________

18. 7,377,844.65̲4 = _______________________________

19. 4,207,963.92̲2 = _______________________________

20. 1,9̲46,867.958 = _______________________________

21. 6,93̲8,711.822 = _______________________________

22. 1,927,0̲68.729 = _______________________________

23. 1,4̲61,975.873 = _______________________________

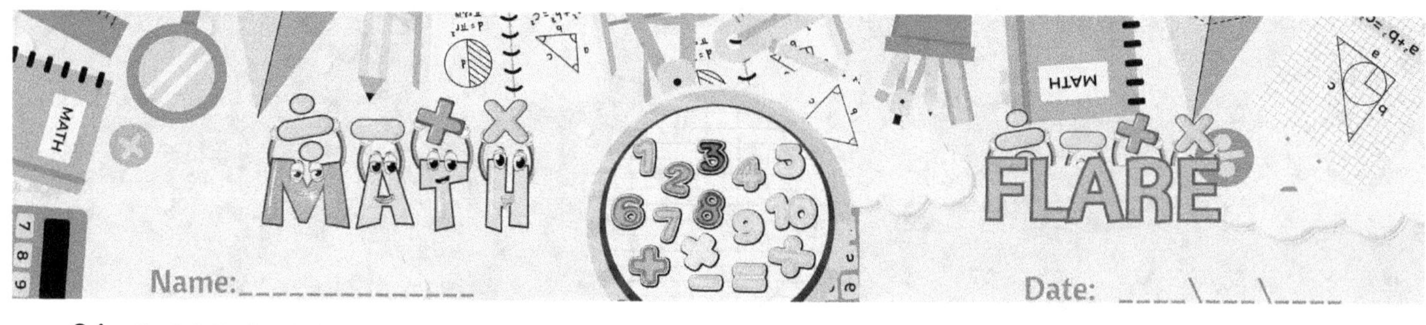

Name:_______________   Date: _______________

24. 2,625,2_1_6.936 = _______________________________

25. 6,096,_7_23.602 = _______________________________

26. 7,_9_81,646.067 = _______________________________

27. 8,488,_3_40.605 = _______________________________

28. 9,930,8_3_4.034 = _______________________________

29. 4,487,_1_81.516 = _______________________________

30. 3,201,120.4_3_4 = _______________________________

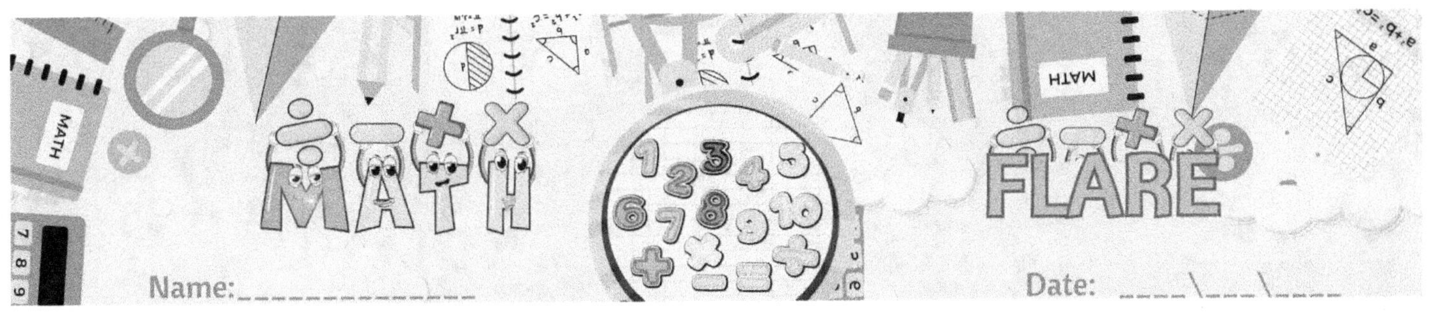

Place Value: Expanded Notation

Provide the expanded notation for each value.

31. _______________________ 7 hundred thousands + 5 ten thousands + 6 thousands + 8 hundreds + 1 ten + 8 ones + 4 tenths + 6 hundredths + 4 thousandths

32. _______________________ 2 hundred thousands + 1 ten thousand + 3 thousands + 4 tens + 5 ones + 9 tenths + 4 hundredths + 1 thousandth

33. _______________________ 9 hundred thousands + 4 ten thousands + 5 thousands + 7 hundreds + 4 tens + 9 ones + 2 tenths + 3 hundredths + 8 thousandths

34. _______________________ 4 hundred thousands + 1 ten thousand + 9 thousands + 1 hundred + 6 tens + 5 ones + 9 tenths + 7 hundredths + 5 thousandths

35. _________________________ 6 hundred thousands + 3 ten thousands + 3 thousands + 6 hundreds + 7 tens + 7 tenths + 2 hundredths + 6 thousandths

36. _________________________ 8 hundred thousands + 8 ten thousands + 3 thousands + 2 hundreds + 1 ten + 7 ones + 4 tenths + 4 hundredths + 4 thousandths

37. _________________________ 6 hundred thousands + 3 ten thousands + 5 thousands + 5 hundreds + 7 ones + 6 tenths + 2 hundredths + 3 thousandths

38. _________________________ 1 hundred thousand + 6 ten thousands + 4 thousands + 5 hundreds + 3 tens + 6 ones + 9 tenths + 6 hundredths + 6 thousandths

39. _______________________   7 hundred thousands + 5 ten thousands + 8 thousands + 3 hundreds + 2 tens + 7 ones + 9 tenths + 8 hundredths + 2 thousandths

40. _______________________   5 hundred thousands + 5 ten thousands + 3 thousands + 7 hundreds + 2 tens + 5 ones + 5 hundredths + 9 thousandths

41. _______________________   5 hundred thousands + 4 ten thousands + 2 thousands + 8 hundreds + 3 tens + 2 ones + 4 tenths + 5 hundredths

42. _______________________   5 hundred thousands + 3 ten thousands + 5 thousands + 5 hundreds + 6 tens + 6 ones + 6 tenths + 7 hundredths + 3 thousandths

43. _________________________ 2 hundred thousands + 9 ten thousands + 3 thousands + 3 hundreds + 4 tens + 9 tenths + 8 hundredths + 4 thousandths

44. _________________________ 9 hundred thousands + 7 ten thousands + 7 thousands + 9 hundreds + 7 tens + 5 ones + 8 tenths + 7 hundredths + 2 thousandths

45. _________________________ 4 hundred thousands + 8 ten thousands + 7 thousands + 4 hundreds + 9 tens + 4 ones + 4 tenths + 1 hundredth + 4 thousandths

46. _________________________ 7 hundred thousands + 6 ten thousands + 5 thousands + 3 hundreds + 6 tens + 3 ones + 1 tenth + 1 hundredth + 6 thousandths

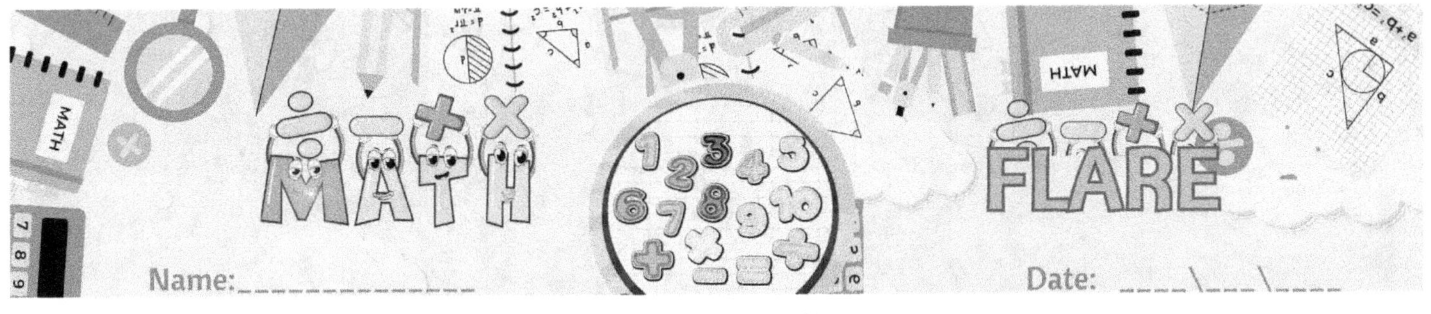

47. _______________________ 9 hundred thousands + 7 ten thousands + 9 hundreds + 2 tens + 9 tenths + 9 hundredths + 2 thousandths

48. _______________________ 2 hundred thousands + 8 ten thousands + 2 thousands + 6 hundreds + 2 tens + 9 ones + 1 tenth + 1 thousandth

49. _______________________ 2 hundred thousands + 2 ten thousands + 4 hundreds + 8 tens + 1 one + 9 hundredths + 4 thousandths

50. _______________________ 7 hundred thousands + 2 ten thousands + 5 thousands + 5 hundreds + 8 tens + 8 ones + 7 tenths + 9 hundredths + 6 thousandths

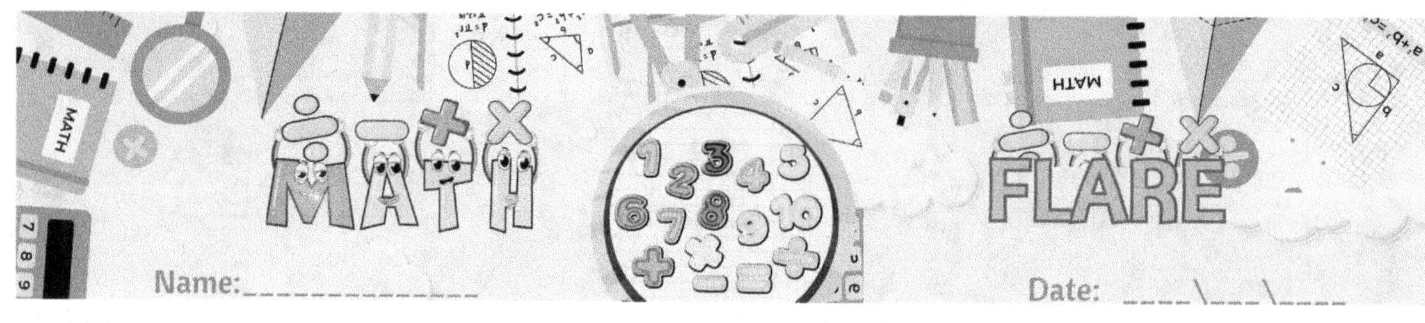

51. _________________________ 4 hundred thousands + 4 ten thousands + 1 thousand + 5 hundreds + 7 tens + 9 ones + 2 tenths + 9 hundredths + 8 thousandths

52. _________________________ 8 hundred thousands + 8 ten thousands + 1 thousand + 3 hundreds + 2 tens + 7 ones + 9 tenths + 8 hundredths + 3 thousandths

53. _________________________ 9 hundred thousands + 3 ten thousands + 3 thousands + 6 hundreds + 4 tens + 5 ones + 1 tenth + 4 hundredths + 9 thousandths

54. _________________________ 4 hundred thousands + 9 ten thousands + 5 hundreds + 9 tens + 8 ones + 8 hundredths + 1 thousandth

55. _______________________________ 1 hundred thousand + 3 ten thousands + 9 thousands + 6 hundreds + 6 tens + 2 ones + 4 tenths + 6 hundredths + 3 thousandths

56. _______________________________ 3 hundred thousands + 3 ten thousands + 7 thousands + 9 hundreds + 8 tens + 4 ones + 2 hundredths + 5 thousandths

57. _______________________________ 8 hundred thousands + 5 ten thousands + 7 thousands + 5 hundreds + 9 tenths + 4 hundredths

58. _______________________________ 2 hundred thousands + 9 ten thousands + 6 thousands + 1 hundred + 1 ten + 6 ones + 7 tenths + 2 hundredths + 3 thousandths

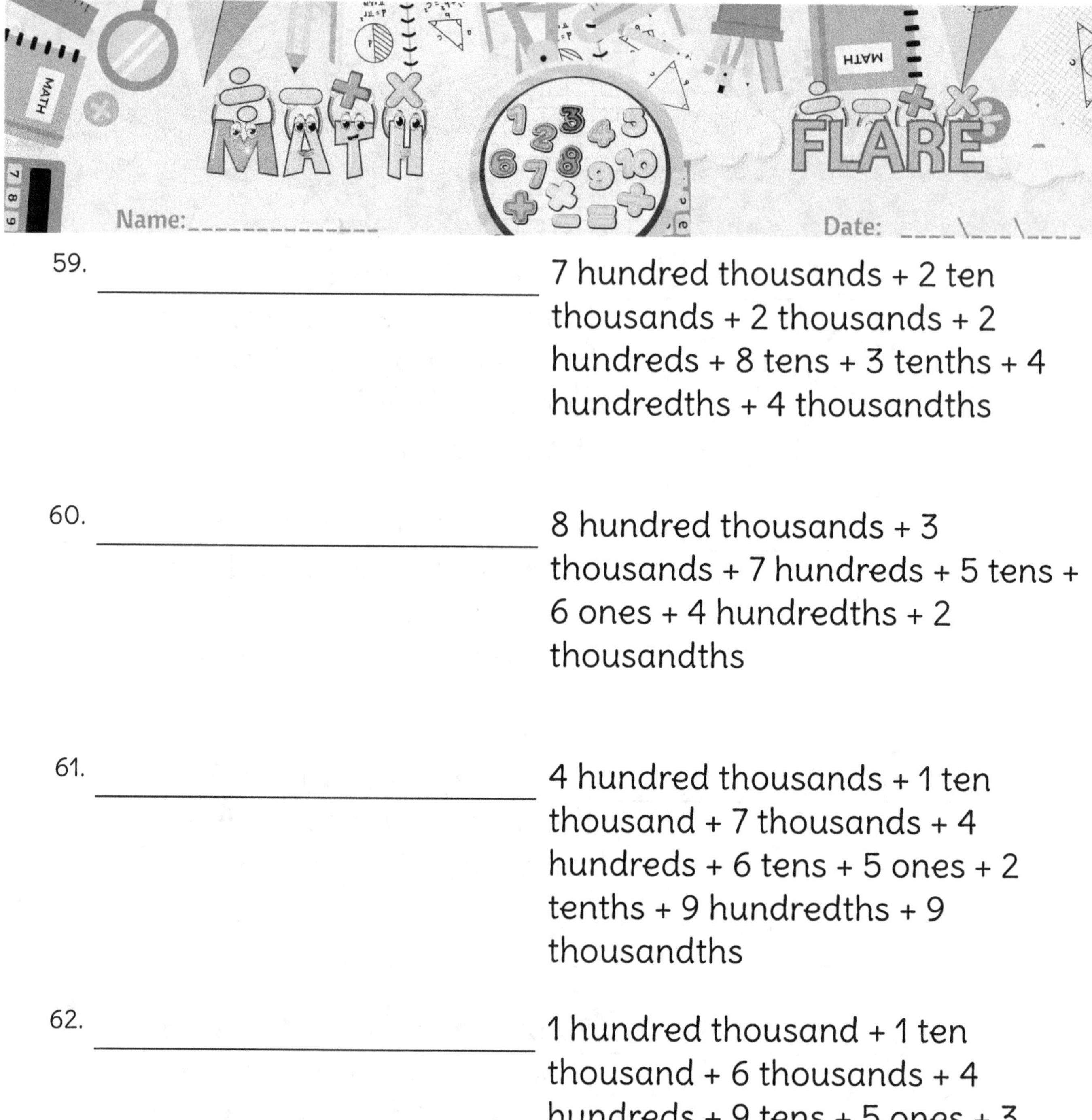

59. _________________________ 7 hundred thousands + 2 ten thousands + 2 thousands + 2 hundreds + 8 tens + 3 tenths + 4 hundredths + 4 thousandths

60. _________________________ 8 hundred thousands + 3 thousands + 7 hundreds + 5 tens + 6 ones + 4 hundredths + 2 thousandths

61. _________________________ 4 hundred thousands + 1 ten thousand + 7 thousands + 4 hundreds + 6 tens + 5 ones + 2 tenths + 9 hundredths + 9 thousandths

62. _________________________ 1 hundred thousand + 1 ten thousand + 6 thousands + 4 hundreds + 9 tens + 5 ones + 3 tenths + 7 hundredths + 1 thousandth

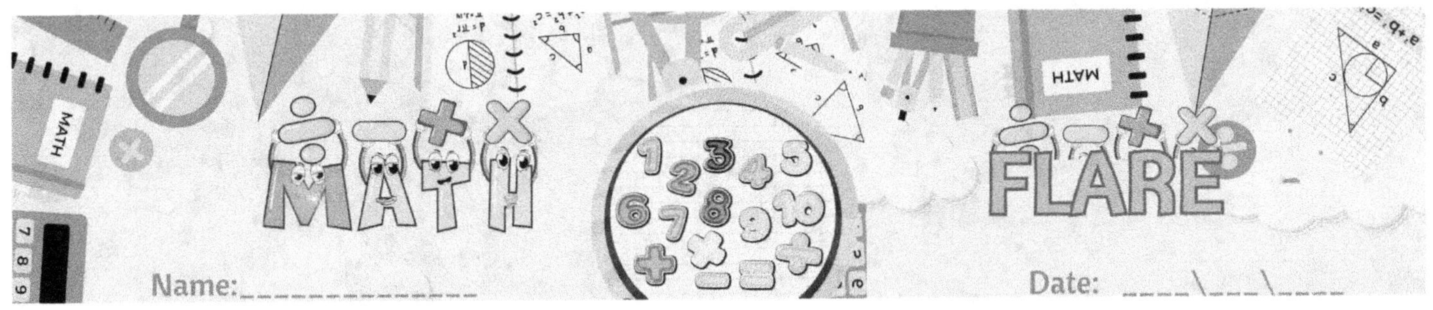

Place Value: Expanded Notation

Provide the expanded notation for each value.

63. 234,283.544 ___________________________________

64. 303,649.311 ___________________________________

65. 598,363.590 ___________________________________

66. 104,101.229 ___________________________________

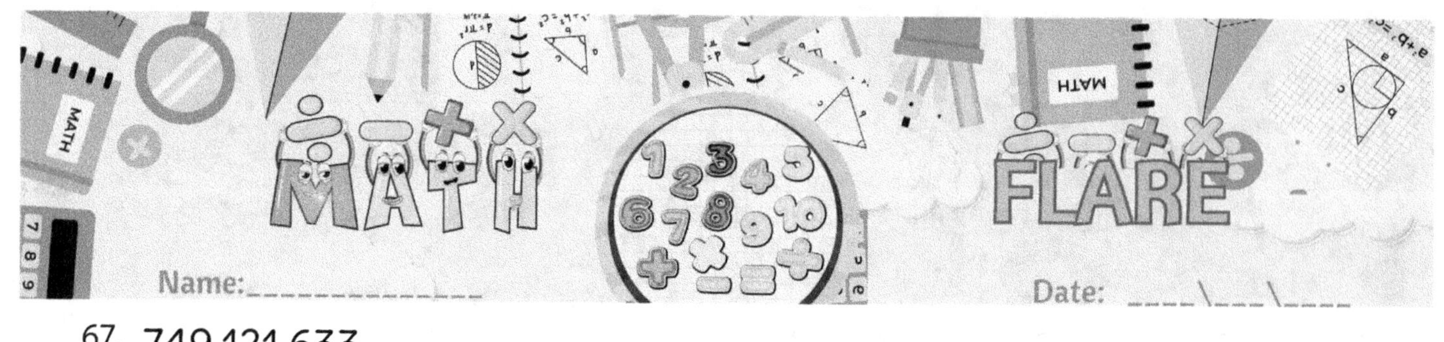

67. 749,121.633

68. 338,267.503

69. 490,549.837

70. 410,999.390

71. 768,919.017

72. 321,714.562 __________________________

73. 762,711.371 __________________________

74. 222,259.945 __________________________

75. 487,185.778 __________________________

76. 433,490.892 __________________________

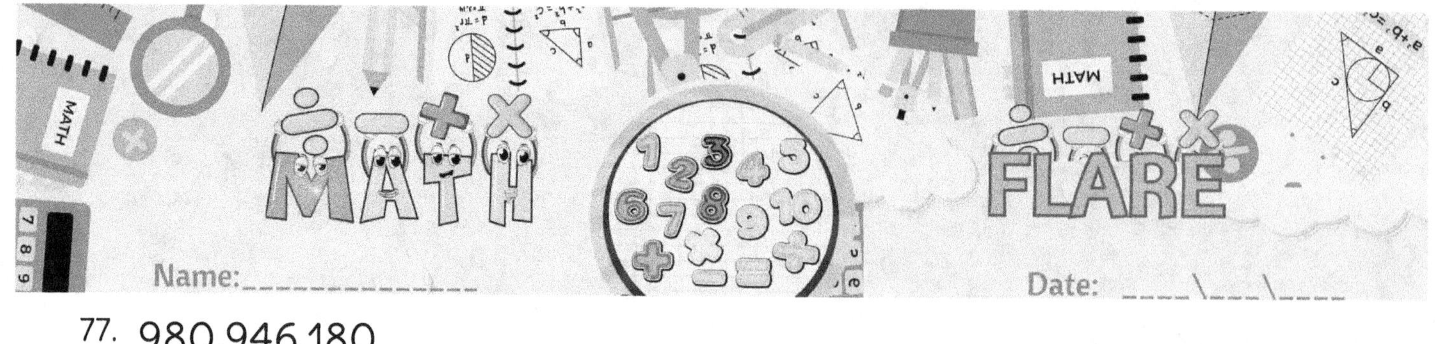

77. 980,946.180 ________________________

78. 401,446.698 ________________________

79. 754,699.291 ________________________

80. 739,388.801 ________________________

81. 144,155.011 ________________________

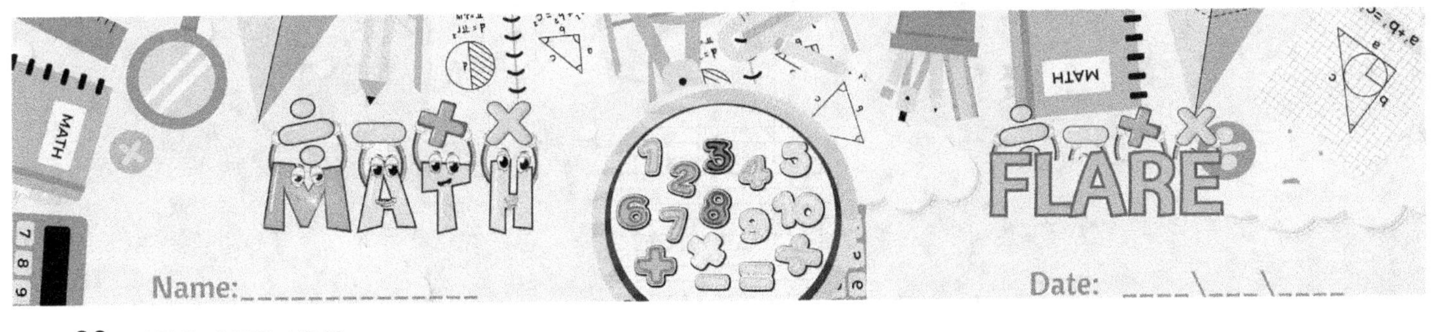

82. 179,187.185

83. 358,353.082

84. 777,853.935

85. 123,301.120

86. 150,362.964

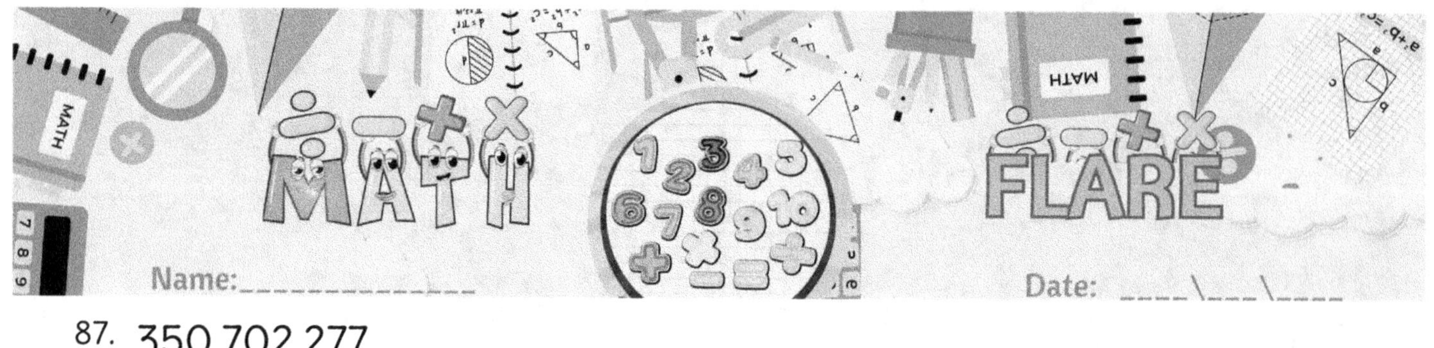

87. 350,702.277 ___________________________

88. 177,035.746 ___________________________

89. 370,956.055 ___________________________

90. 974,119.136 ___________________________

91. 861,589.948 ___________________________

Place Value: Expanded Notation

Provide the expanded notation for each value.

92. _________________________ 600,000 + 70,000 + 2,000 + 80 + 5 + 0.8 + 0.08 + 0.008

93. _________________________ 900,000 + 60,000 + 7,000 + 300 + 10 + 1 + 0.4 + 0.04 + 0.007

94. _________________________ 500,000 + 10,000 + 6,000 + 400 + 30 + 0.7

95. _________________________ 500,000 + 40,000 + 9,000 + 400 + 9 + 0.4 + 0.04 + 0.001

96. _________________________ 300,000 + 10,000 + 7,000 + 800 + 40 + 2 + 0.4 + 0.09 + 0.009

97. _________________________ $600,000 + 30,000 + 3,000 + 200 + 20 + 2 + 0.1 + 0.07 + 0.003$

98. _________________________ $400,000 + 7,000 + 900 + 30 + 2 + 0.3 + 0.003$

99. _________________________ $200,000 + 90,000 + 5,000 + 800 + 50 + 2 + 0.9 + 0.08$

100. _________________________ $600,000 + 70,000 + 2,000 + 400 + 20 + 4 + 0.2 + 0.02 + 0.008$

101. _________________________ $100,000 + 40,000 + 6,000 + 300 + 90 + 8 + 0.6$

102. _________________________ $900,000 + 70,000 + 7,000 + 800 + 10 + 3 + 0.7 + 0.01 + 0.003$

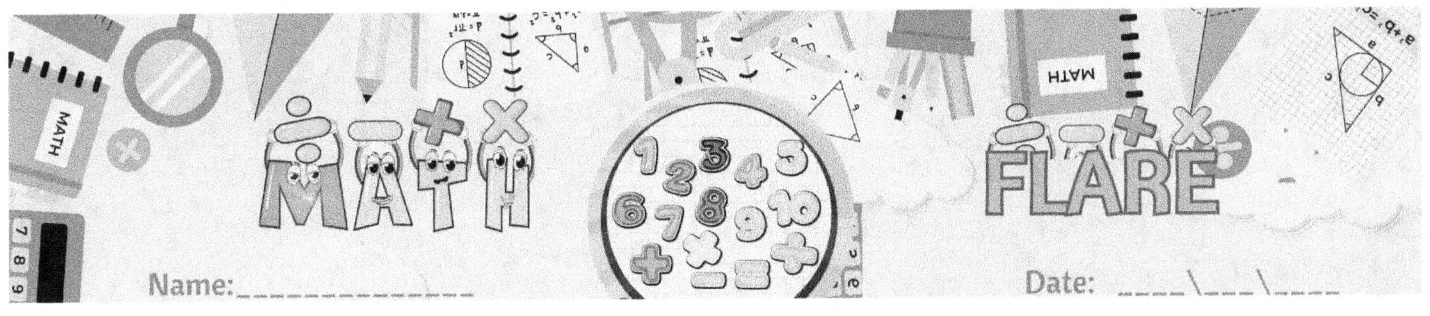

103. _________________________ $500,000 + 90,000 + 9,000 + 30 + 4 + 0.6 + 0.07 + 0.001$

104. _________________________ $700,000 + 30,000 + 7,000 + 800 + 40 + 9 + 0.2 + 0.02 + 0.007$

105. _________________________ $300,000 + 90,000 + 5,000 + 700 + 80 + 5 + 0.9 + 0.02 + 0.003$

106. _________________________ $500,000 + 20,000 + 4,000 + 500 + 60 + 6 + 0.8 + 0.02 + 0.008$

107. _________________________ $600,000 + 30,000 + 3,000 + 200 + 7 + 0.6 + 0.08 + 0.004$

108. _________________________ $900,000 + 30,000 + 8,000 + 300 + 50 + 0.6 + 0.006$

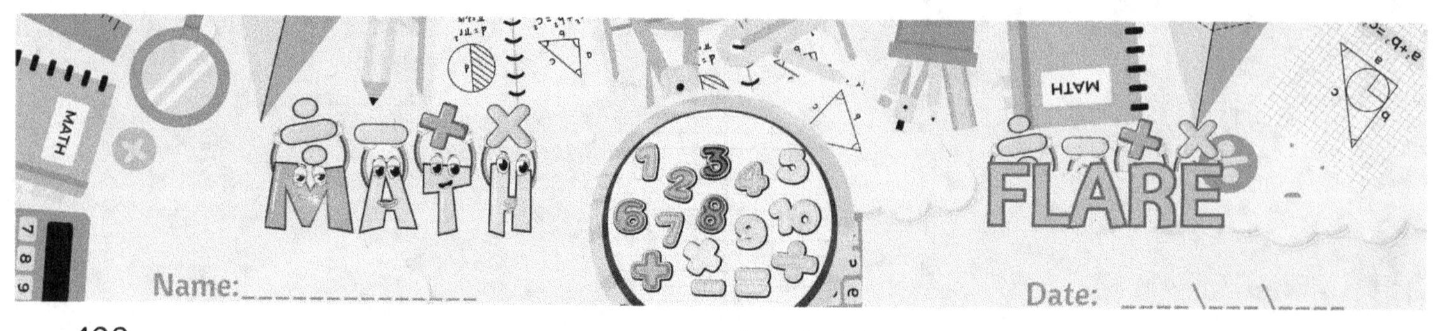

109. _________________________ 700,000 + 20,000 + 300 + 50 + 6
+ 0.6 + 0.09 + 0.001

110. _________________________ 300,000 + 60,000 + 7,000 + 900
+ 40 + 0.4 + 0.05

111. _________________________ 500,000 + 50,000 + 8,000 + 400
+ 30 + 7 + 0.9 + 0.09 + 0.005

112. _________________________ 200,000 + 60,000 + 7,000 + 200
+ 70 + 9 + 0.1 + 0.01 + 0.004

113. _________________________ 400,000 + 80,000 + 2,000 + 100
+ 70 + 3 + 0.5 + 0.07 + 0.003

114. _________________________ 200,000 + 20,000 + 7,000 + 600
+ 80 + 0.6 + 0.01 + 0.002

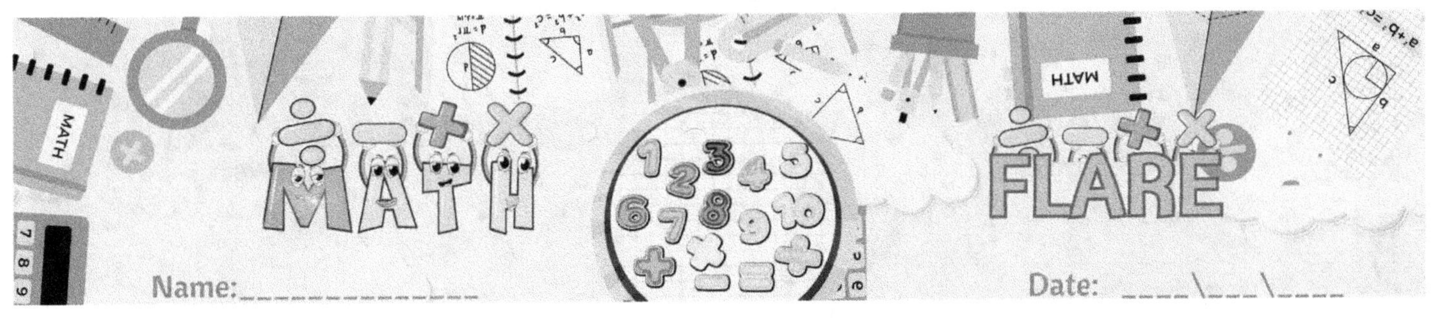

115. __________________________   100,000 + 20,000 + 6,000 + 700
+ 10 + 3 + 0.8 + 0.01 + 0.001

116. __________________________   900,000 + 90,000 + 9,000 + 900
+ 40 + 7 + 0.8 + 0.06 + 0.002

117. __________________________   500,000 + 60,000 + 4,000 + 800
+ 50 + 5 + 0.8 + 0.06 + 0.007

118. __________________________   500,000 + 40,000 + 5,000 + 700
+ 10 + 1 + 0.1 + 0.02 + 0.004

119. __________________________   400,000 + 6,000 + 900 + 8 + 0.4
+ 0.09 + 0.008

120. __________________________   800,000 + 4,000 + 600 + 7 + 0.2
+ 0.09 + 0.004

Place Value: Expanded Notation

Provide the expanded notation for each value.

121. 442,932.527 _______________________________

122. 523,394.267 _______________________________

123. 434,269.227 _______________________________

124. 513,247.337 _______________________________

125. 267,427.868 _______________________________

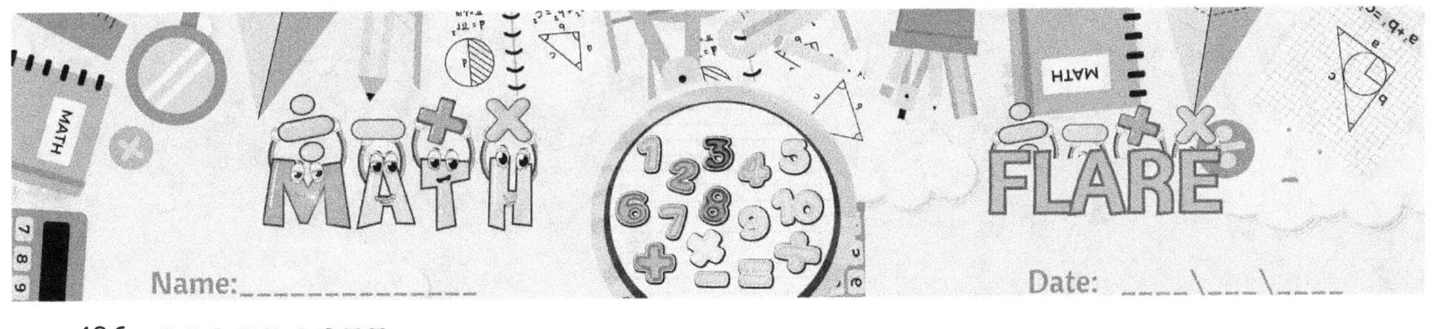

126. 889,736.235 _______________________________

127. 255,844.359 _______________________________

128. 904,140.967 _______________________________

129. 479,807.251 _______________________________

130. 912,505.129 _______________________________

131. 355,297.154 _______________________________

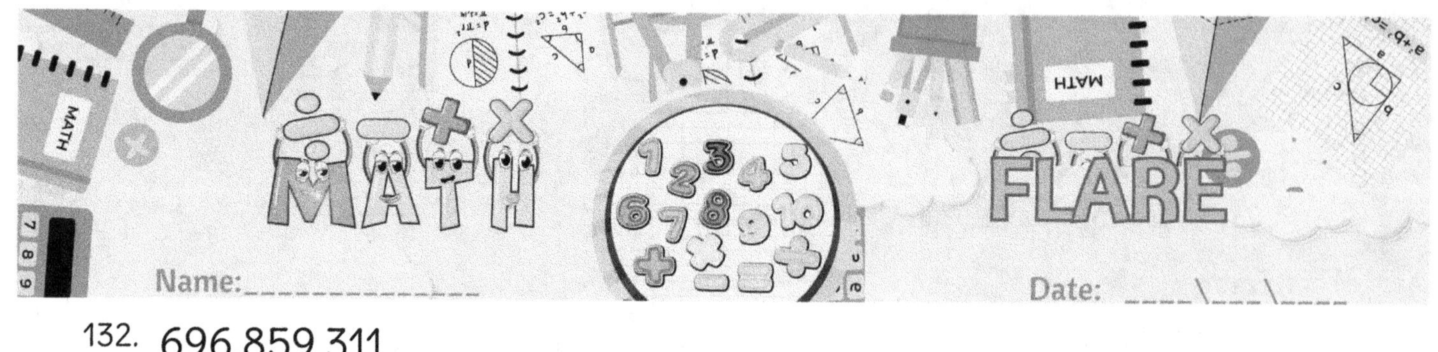

132. 696,859.311 ___________________________

133. 679,983.958 ___________________________

134. 957,829.258 ___________________________

135. 792,216.948 ___________________________

136. 857,040.502 ___________________________

137. 933,606.302 ___________________________

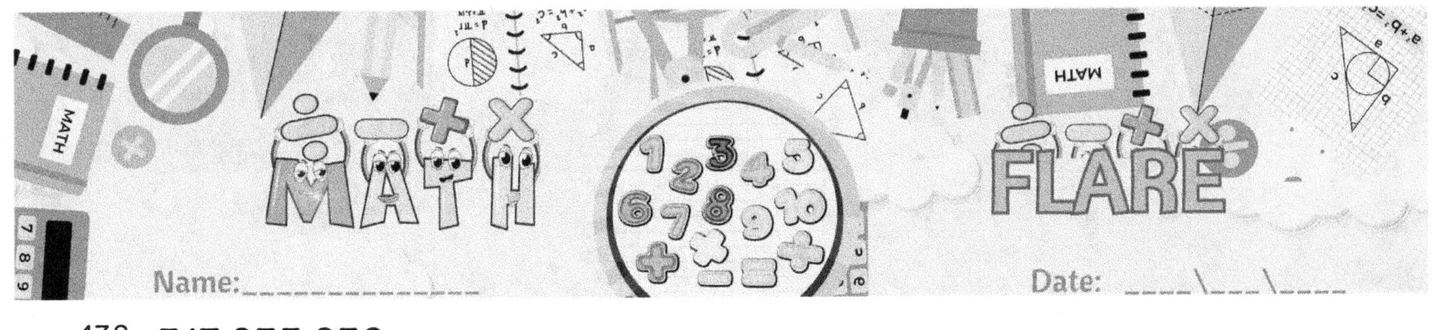

138. 317,835.839

139. 258,183.702

140. 881,598.894

141. 125,870.793

142. 391,776.077

143. 376,640.754

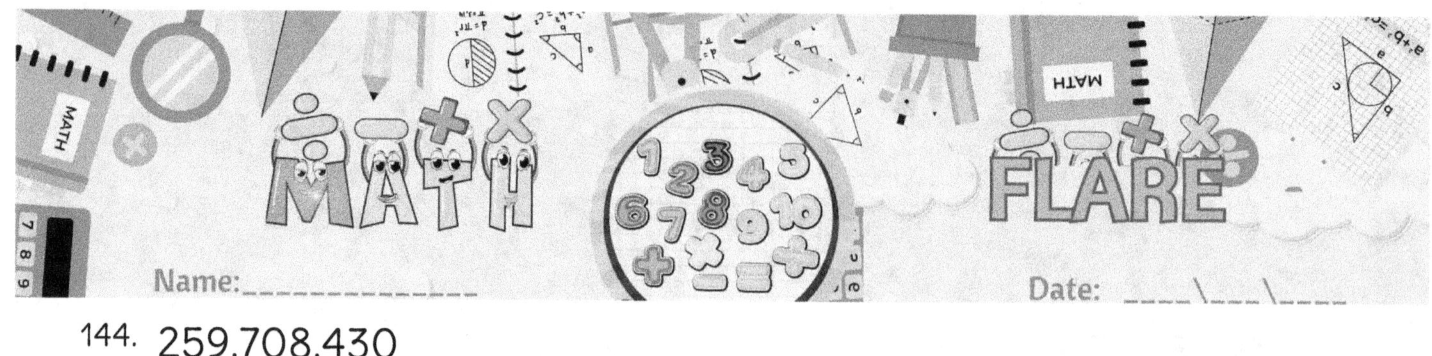

144. 259,708.430 _______________________

145. 356,843.432 _______________________

146. 423,407.994 _______________________

147. 573,056.383 _______________________

148. 403,329.629 _______________________

149. 205,712.194 _______________________

Place Value: Expanded Notation

Provide the expanded notation for each value.

150. _________________________ six hundred twenty-three thousand seventeen and six hundred seventy-four thousandths

151. _________________________ six hundred fifty-one thousand one hundred fifty-eight and three hundred forty-six thousandths

152. _________________________ six hundred seventy-two thousand seven hundred six and three hundred thirty-five thousandths

153. _________________________ eight hundred thirty-seven thousand two hundred eighty-four and two hundred seventy-four thousandths

154. _______________________ six hundred seventy-four thousand eight hundred twelve and three hundred twenty-four thousandths

155. _______________________ eight hundred sixty-three thousand four hundred fifty-four and six hundred sixty-seven thousandths

156. _______________________ one hundred fifty-eight thousand two hundred thirty-five and eight hundred seventy-four thousandths

157. _______________________ four hundred seven thousand six hundred sixty-six and eight hundred sixty-five thousandths

158. _______________________ seven hundred three thousand six hundred thirty-four and seven hundred twenty-six thousandths

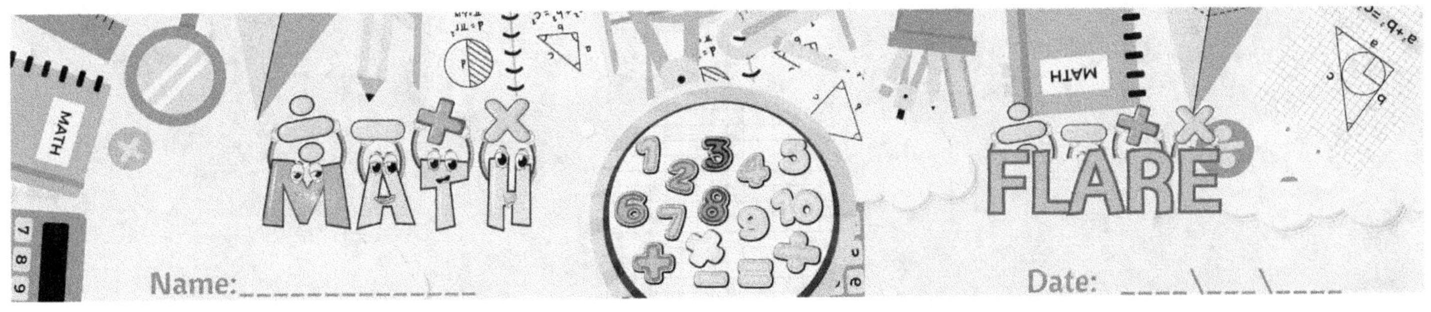

159. _______________________ two hundred sixteen thousand three hundred fifty-three and seven hundred eighty-three thousandths

160. _______________________ two hundred forty-three thousand one hundred twenty-nine and seven hundred twenty-three thousandths

161. _______________________ six hundred eighty-four thousand four hundred ninety-five and eight hundred sixty thousandths

162. _______________________ six hundred five thousand nine hundred one and seven thousandths

163. _______________________ seven hundred ten thousand nine hundred ninety-seven and two hundred nineteen thousandths

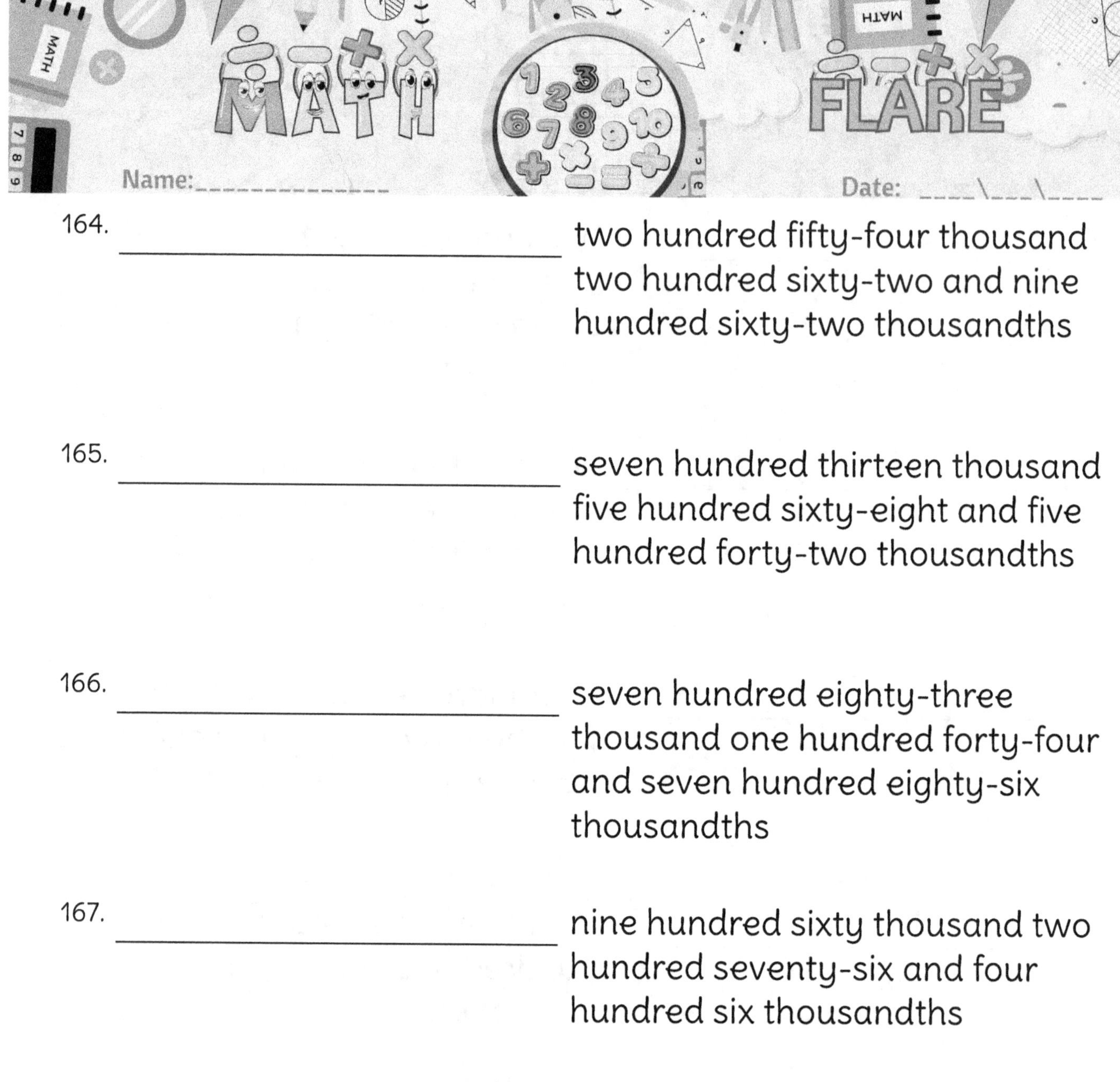

164. _________________________ two hundred fifty-four thousand two hundred sixty-two and nine hundred sixty-two thousandths

165. _________________________ seven hundred thirteen thousand five hundred sixty-eight and five hundred forty-two thousandths

166. _________________________ seven hundred eighty-three thousand one hundred forty-four and seven hundred eighty-six thousandths

167. _________________________ nine hundred sixty thousand two hundred seventy-six and four hundred six thousandths

168. _________________________ three hundred seventeen thousand three hundred forty-five and one hundred eighty-eight thousandth

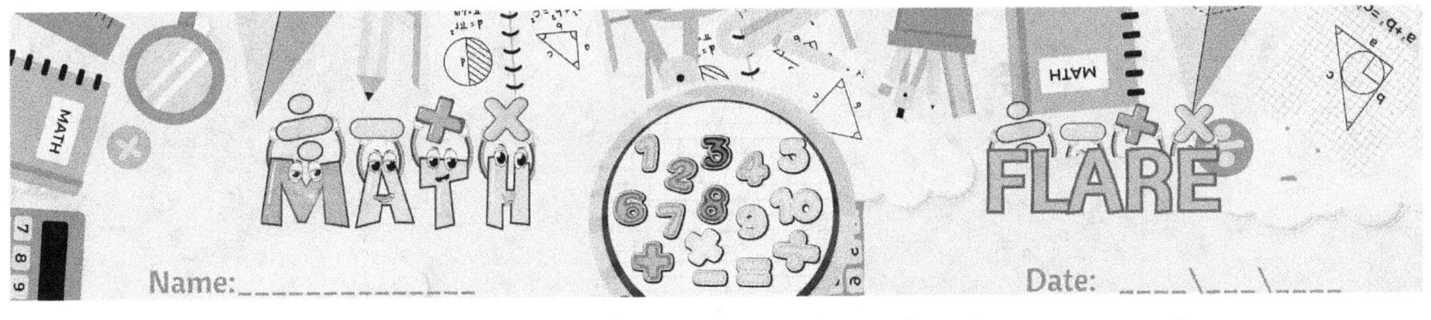

169. _________________________ three hundred seventy-six thousand one hundred ninety-two and five hundred eighty-one thousandths

170. _________________________ five hundred ninety-eight thousand five hundred fifty-four and eight hundred forty thousandths

171. _________________________ two hundred fifty-two thousand one hundred sixty-five and ninety-one thousandths

172. _________________________ seven hundred six thousand eight hundred eighty-three and seven hundred forty-nine thousandths

173. _________________________ three hundred twenty-four thousand four hundred fifty and six hundred twenty-four thousandths

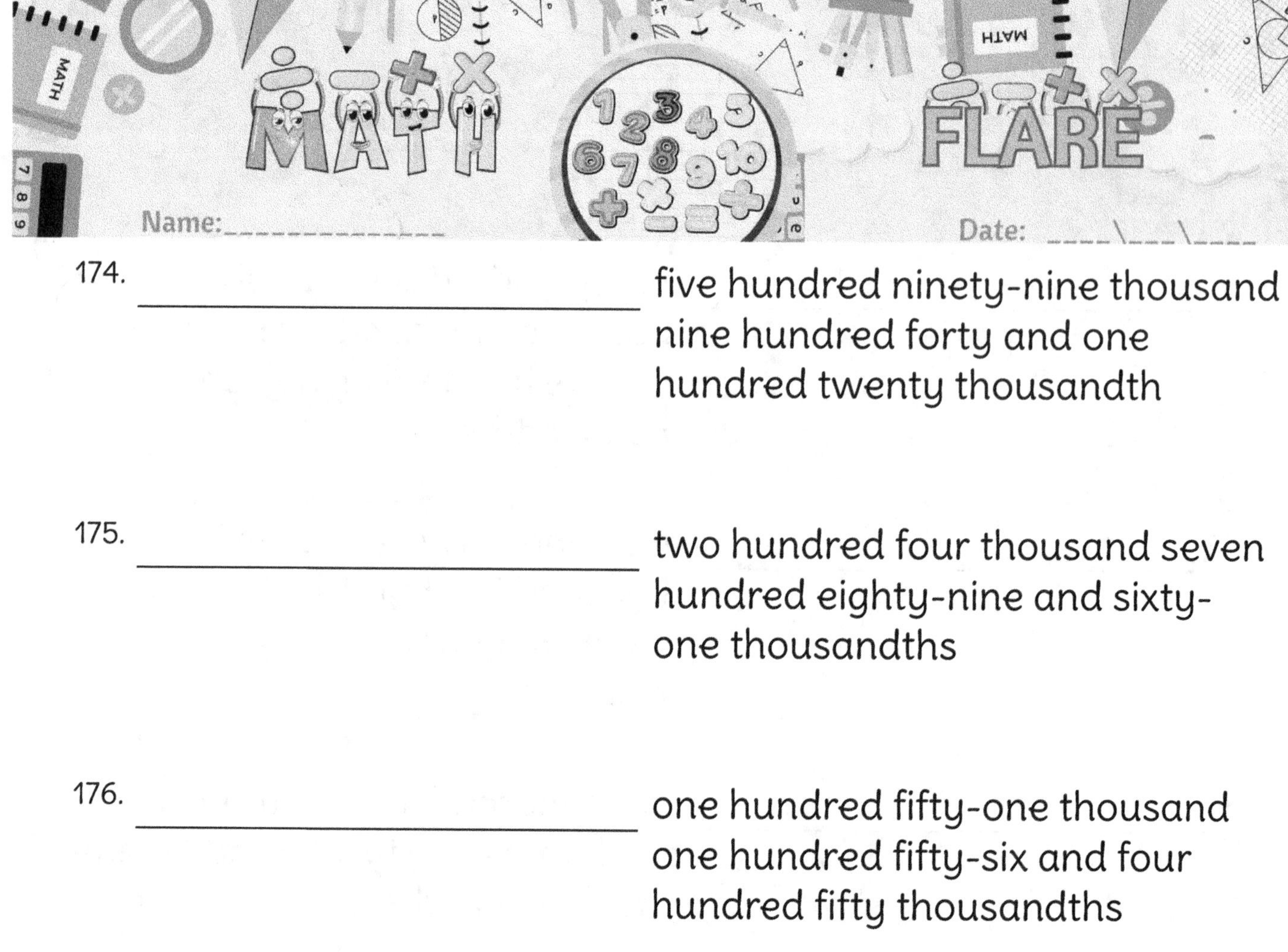

174. _________________________ five hundred ninety-nine thousand nine hundred forty and one hundred twenty thousandth

175. _________________________ two hundred four thousand seven hundred eighty-nine and sixty-one thousandths

176. _________________________ one hundred fifty-one thousand one hundred fifty-six and four hundred fifty thousandths

177. _________________________ two hundred forty-six thousand seven hundred fifty-three and five hundred thirteen thousandths

178. _________________________ two hundred seventy-four thousand five hundred sixty and seven hundred ninety-seven thousandths

Place Value: Expanded Notation

Provide the expanded notation for each value.

179. 256,403.905 ___________________________________

180. 844,019.873 ___________________________________

181. 416,679.852 ___________________________________

182. 852,514.729 ___________________________________

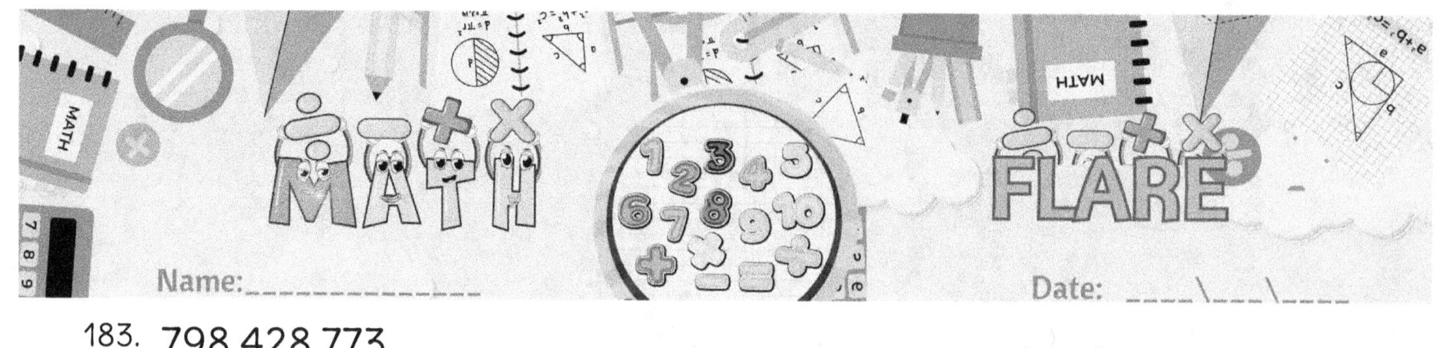

183. 798,428.773

184. 856,789.575

185. 361,346.783

186. 682,590.818

187. 859,575.036

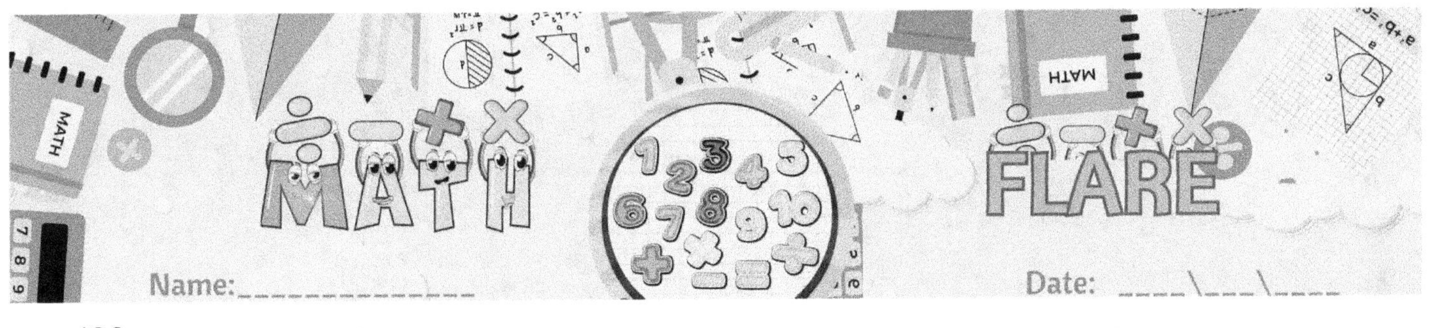

188. 105,171.634

189. 194,374.591

190. 733,981.074

191. 549,373.638

192. 329,971.576

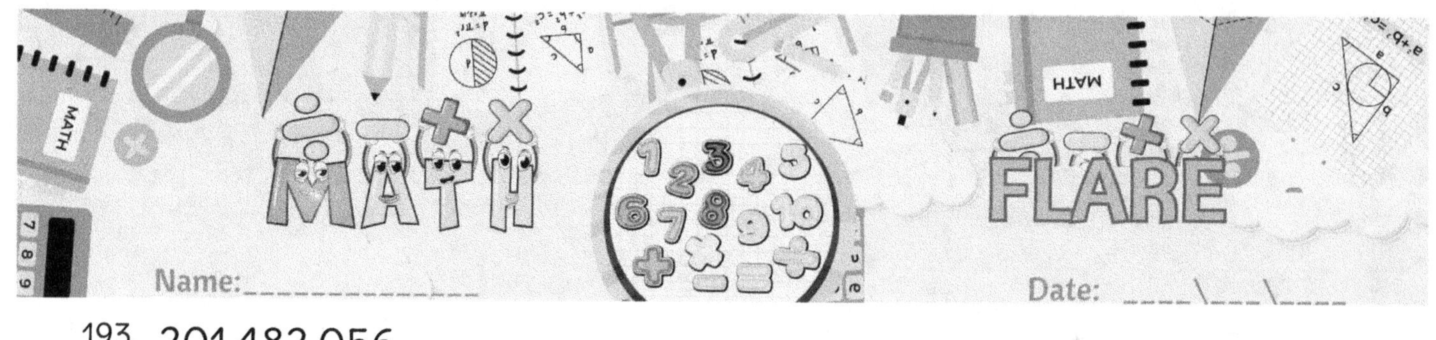

193. 201,482.056

194. 115,053.979

195. 297,103.035

196. 519,969.785

197. 680,778.857

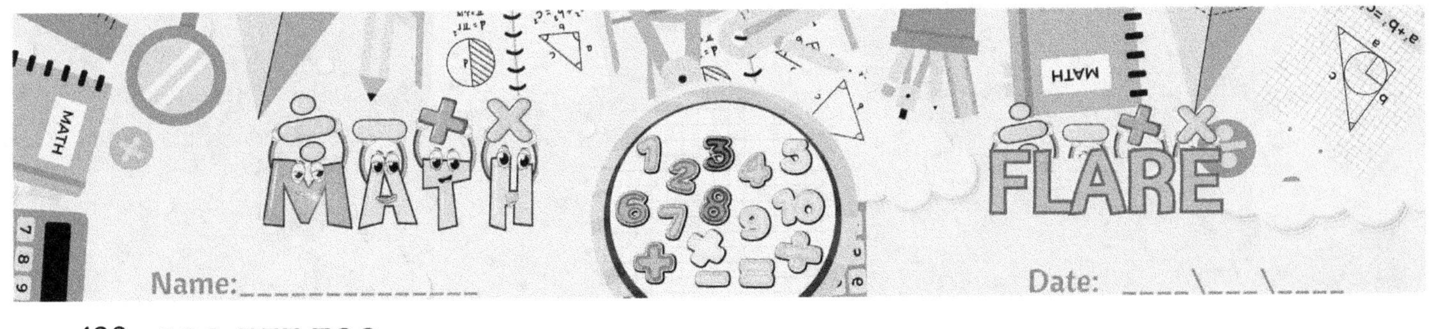

198. 222,377.792 _______________________

199. 546,139.888 _______________________

200. 573,698.644 _______________________

201. 463,131.587 _______________________

202. 355,711.195 _______________________

203. 127,137.048

204. 607,157.353

205. 470,852.583

206. 944,274.596

207. 448,255.711

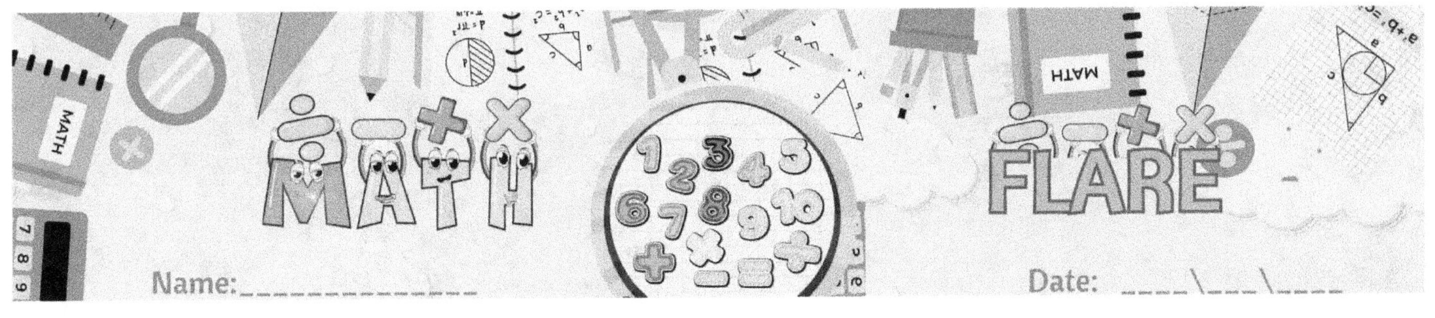

208. 337,344.154 _______________________________________

209. 570,023.262 _______________________________________

210. 812,298.217 _______________________________________

211. 911,482.360 _______________________________________

212. 233,106.068 _______________________________________

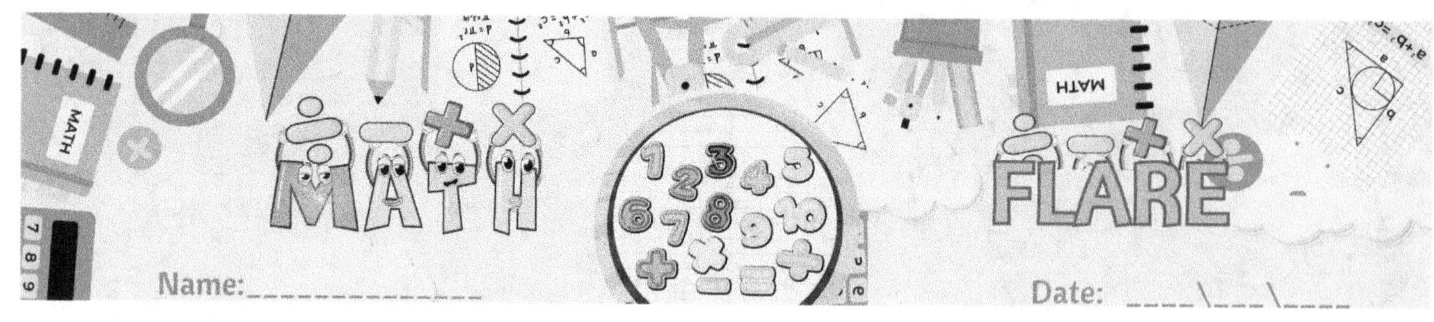

Rounding Numbers
Round to the underlined digit.

213. 5,472,308.209 = _____________

214. 3,723,339.090 = _____________

215. 8,264,498.712 = _____________

216. 8,319,811.306 = _____________

217. 8,074,722.337 = _____________

218. 8,542,076.433 = _____________

219. 8,929,161.791 = _____________

220. 1,309,777.238 = _____________

221. 9,235,697.499 = _____________

222. 9,551,047.730 = _____________

223. 2,229,705.972 = _____________

224. 6,422,115.068 = _____________

225. 1,491,812.024 = _____________

226. 9,221,935.156 = _____________

227. 6,0<u>5</u>4,016.937 = _____________

228. 3,093,9<u>6</u>6.452 = _____________

229. <u>4</u>,028,370.859 = _____________

230. 6,<u>8</u>48,192.758 = _____________

231. 4,703,775.<u>9</u>25 = _____________

232. 1,2<u>4</u>3,757.219 = _____________

233. 7,284,20<u>9</u>.085 = _____________

234. 6,827,<u>0</u>52.605 = _____________

235. 4,80<u>8</u>,882.866 = _____________

236. 1,609,686.<u>5</u>74 = _____________

237. 8,253,77<u>6</u>.821 = _____________

238. 2,912,71<u>4</u>.204 = _____________

239. <u>4</u>,859,369.931 = _____________

240. 4,<u>1</u>70,721.860 = _____________

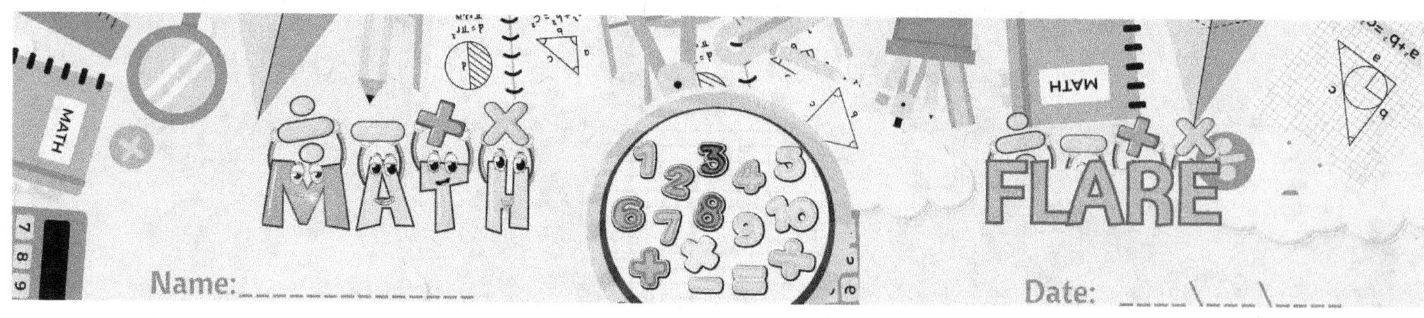

241. 3,343,351.071 = _____________

242. 6,222,308.827 = _____________

243. 5,351,483.712 = _____________

244. 3,820,763.736 = _____________

245. 8,224,987.142 = _____________

246. 4,162,675.698 = _____________

247. 7,827,407.549 = _____________

248. 8,291,481.471 = _____________

249. 2,886,041.072 = _____________

250. 4,651,219.041 = _____________

251. 7,124,975.518 = _____________

252. 8,265,712.139 = _____________

253. 3,294,616.125 = _____________

254. 5,151,621.644 = _____________

255. 6,501,288.9_49 = ___________

256. _5,080,268.141 = ___________

257. 2,3_27,405.976 = ___________

258. 4,849,2_55.409 = ___________

259. 5,5_79,761.509 = ___________

260. 5,4_86,590.675 = ___________

261. 4,388,7_29.031 = ___________

262. 2,3_88,590.663 = ___________

263. 9,3_45,070.682 = ___________

264. 8,85_2,039.870 = ___________

265. 4,_419,206.251 = ___________

266. 8,871,066.3_84 = ___________

267. 5,0_46,851.597 = ___________

268. 8,645,255.6_03 = ___________

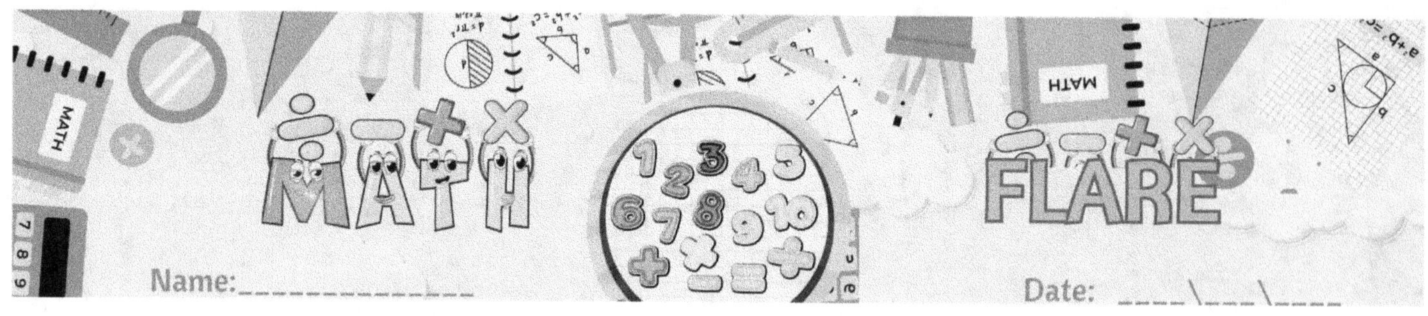

269. 8,9<u>1</u>4,456.224 = _______________

270. 7,654,812.1<u>3</u>9 = _______________

271. 1,066,<u>0</u>34.486 = _______________

272. 6,162,0<u>0</u>8.133 = _______________

273. 4,682,70<u>6</u>.502 = _______________

274. 5,758,439.9<u>3</u>0 = _______________

275. 7,<u>9</u>66,426.165 = _______________

276. 4,013,3<u>8</u>8.672 = _______________

277. 5,199,<u>5</u>64.018 = _______________

278. 8,408,942.2<u>3</u>5 = _______________

279. 8,<u>1</u>97,127.925 = _______________

280. 7,329,1<u>3</u>6.325 = _______________

281. 2,3<u>9</u>4,527.607 = _______________

282. 7,762,<u>5</u>35.465 = _______________

283. 1,207,925.3_79 = ___________

284. 9,377,151.8_17 = ___________

285. 9,723,217.2_39 = ___________

286. 6,43_8,063.784 = ___________

287. 7,9_49,141.093 = ___________

288. 3,13_2,587.441 = ___________

289. 1,325,7_63.656 = ___________

290. 9,7_28,614.724 = ___________

291. 9,282,28_0.597 = ___________

292. _4,404,521.412 = ___________

293. 7,33_2,952.693 = ___________

294. 9,372,779.2_55 = ___________

295. 9,781,99_2.829 = ___________

296. _1,954,760.408 = ___________

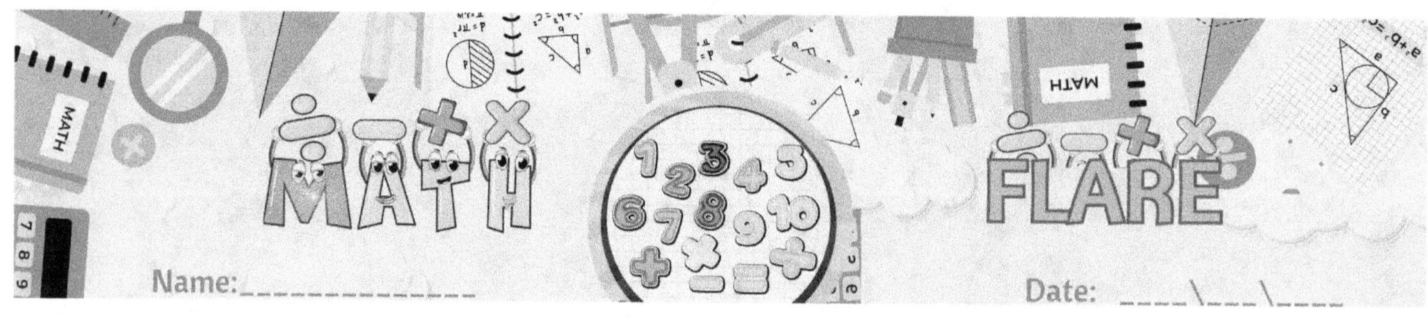

297. 6,877,238.1<u>4</u>4 = _______________

298. 6,4<u>9</u>9,443.841 = _______________

299. 9,401,55<u>7</u>.484 = _______________

300. 9,3<u>5</u>3,920.757 = _______________

301. 9,115,82<u>4</u>.101 = _______________

302. 9,182,1<u>5</u>1.944 = _______________

303. 9,3<u>7</u>7,025.246 = _______________

304. 5,231,22<u>8</u>.933 = _______________

305. 4,585,184.<u>5</u>55 = _______________

306. 1,962,9<u>6</u>7.385 = _______________

307. 4,583,0<u>0</u>5.637 = _______________

308. 7,<u>5</u>36,176.194 = _______________

309. 7,1<u>8</u>5,195.478 = _______________

310. 3,4<u>8</u>7,900.277 = _______________

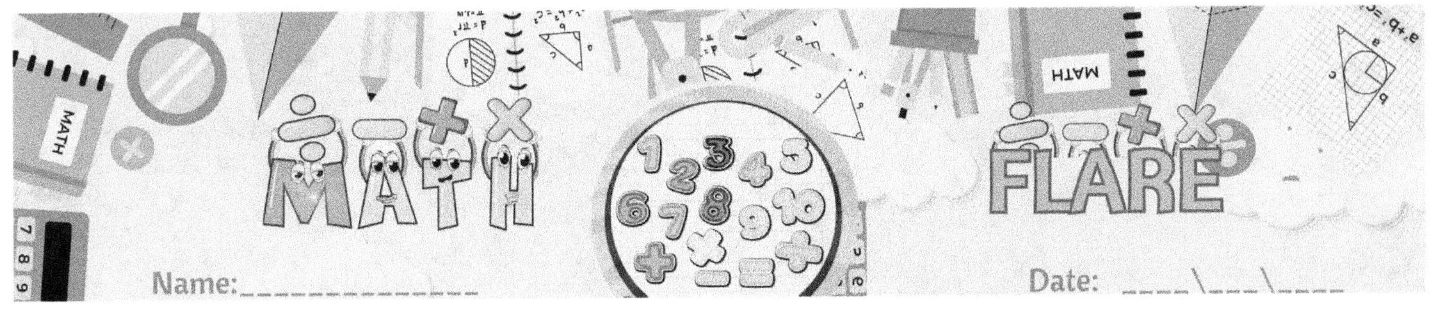

311. 9,880,704.122 = _____________

312. 3,918,463.740 = _____________

313. 6,652,127.483 = _____________

314. 8,250,625.183 = _____________

315. 4,092,063.068 = _____________

316. 6,626,193.564 = _____________

317. 2,180,665.284 = _____________

318. 9,967,918.864 = _____________

319. 9,128,822.630 = _____________

320. 7,981,142.466 = _____________

321. 1,921,925.291 = _____________

322. 2,914,264.156 = _____________

323. 8,319,491.947 = _____________

324. 9,185,841.499 = _____________

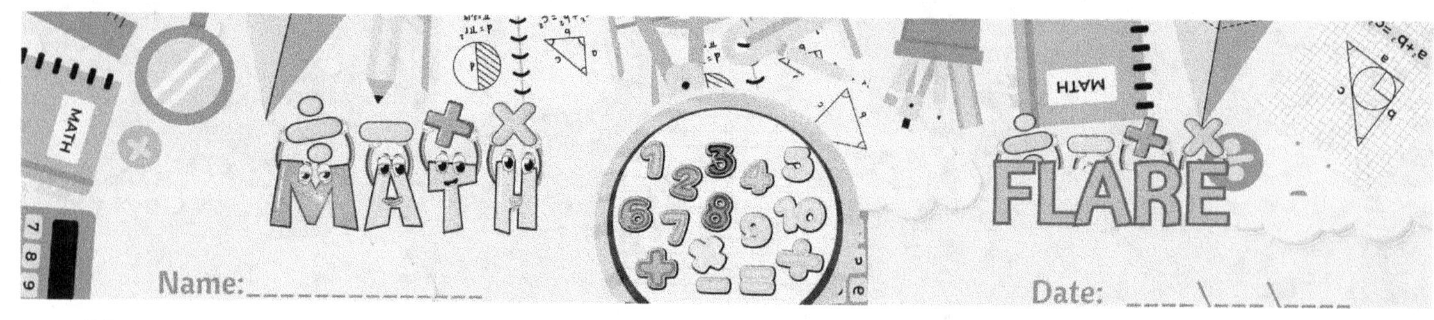

325. 8,372,531.541 = __________ 326. 6,661,513.073 = __________

327. 8,829,055.439 = __________ 328. 5,309,927.246 = __________

329. 5,976,447.101 = __________ 330. 7,011,665.758 = __________

331. 7,136,150.527 = __________ 332. 8,700,120.176 = __________

333. 9,007,384.750 = __________ 334. 8,843,207.167 = __________

335. 8,213,312.223 = __________ 336. 3,212,375.662 = __________

337. 8,385,510.218 = __________ 338. 5,976,696.446 = __________

339. 5,791,967.2<u>6</u>2 = _____________

340. 8,7<u>6</u>0,249.854 = _____________

341. 2,855,058.<u>1</u>47 = _____________

342. 1,412,964.8<u>9</u>9 = _____________

343. 5,<u>9</u>47,391.963 = _____________

344. 7,83<u>7</u>,863.378 = _____________

345. 9,847,910.<u>6</u>01 = _____________

346. 6,363,<u>8</u>16.856 = _____________

347. 7,752,3<u>9</u>3.928 = _____________

348. 9,082,32<u>7</u>.509 = _____________

349. 6,280,716.<u>1</u>87 = _____________

350. 4,155,<u>7</u>99.265 = _____________

351. 9,774,09<u>5</u>.123 = _____________

352. 6,909,3<u>1</u>9.279 = _____________

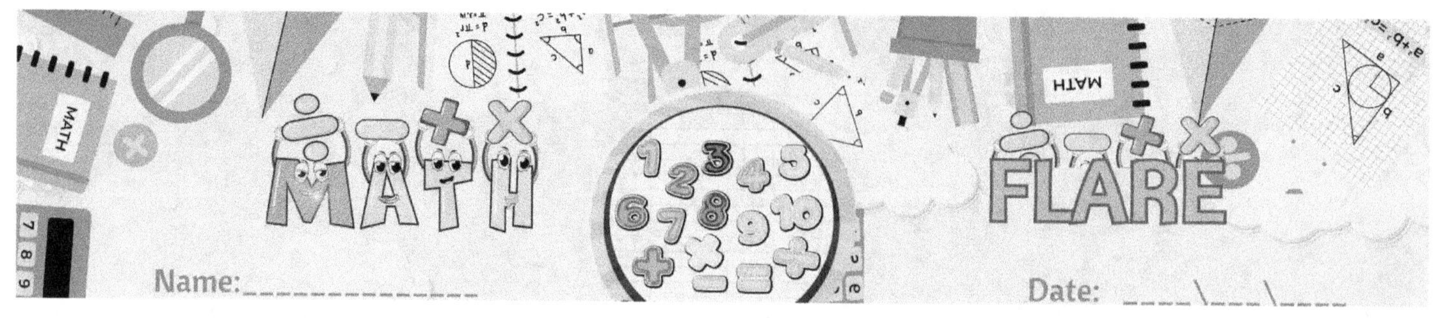

Name: _______________   Date: ____________

353. 7,370,621.2<u>0</u>9 = _____________

354. <u>2</u>,420,415.019 = _____________

355. 8,431,99<u>5</u>.465 = _____________

356. 7,201,559.9<u>4</u>5 = _____________

357. 1,8<u>6</u>2,659.997 = _____________

358. 1,1<u>9</u>1,183.747 = _____________

359. 6,858,<u>6</u>97.391 = _____________

360. 7,923,<u>6</u>71.481 = _____________

361. 3,13<u>3</u>,911.945 = _____________

362. 9,273,0<u>7</u>8.390 = _____________

363. 2,559,729.<u>0</u>93 = _____________

364. 1,<u>1</u>73,529.720 = _____________

365. 6,351,<u>7</u>49.749 = _____________

366. 2,1<u>8</u>0,583.946 = _____________

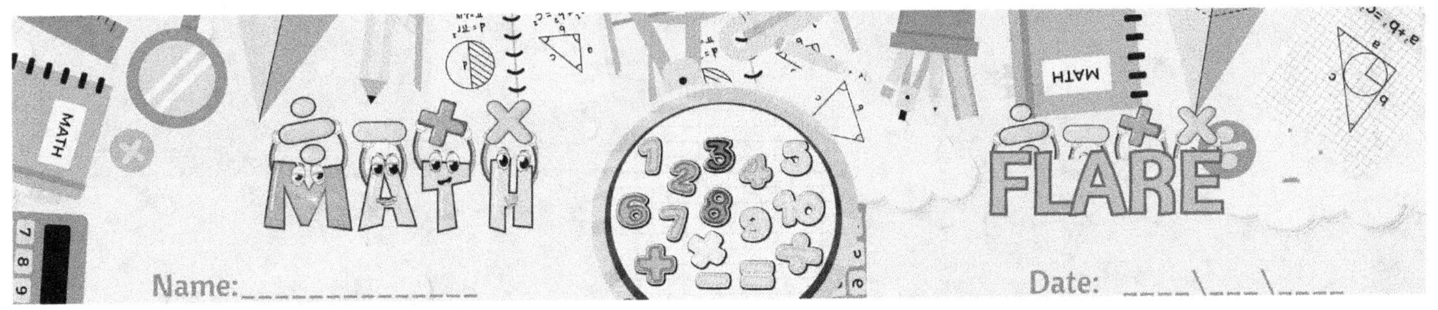

367. 4,911,078.989 = _____________

368. 7,808,920.314 = _____________

369. 1,037,312.960 = _____________

370. 1,879,687.406 = _____________

371. 8,240,683.345 = _____________

372. 6,203,968.837 = _____________

373. 5,175,951.602 = _____________

374. 1,368,572.776 = _____________

375. 6,126,084.319 = _____________

376. 1,508,960.393 = _____________

377. 6,966,872.192 = _____________

378. 1,481,628.569 = _____________

379. 9,337,930.897 = _____________

380. 3,008,714.685 = _____________

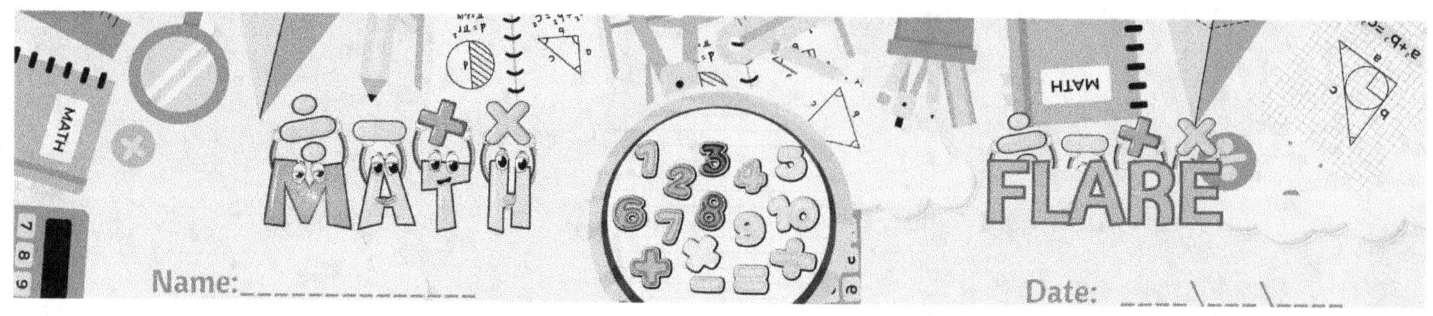

381. 8,909,119.143 = _____________

382. 9,746,727.928 = _____________

383. 9,029,211.058 = _____________

384. 2,820,647.836 = _____________

385. 7,237,570.634 = _____________

386. 1,226,831.248 = _____________

387. 2,329,498.967 = _____________

388. 7,586,969.731 = _____________

389. 1,411,211.702 = _____________

390. 2,011,752.278 = _____________

391. 2,349,715.665 = _____________

392. 8,194,326.471 = _____________

393. 9,117,999.054 = _____________

394. 7,868,295.780 = _____________

ANSWERS

Page 1: Place Value

1. 7 millions

2. 6 ten thousands

3. 2 thousandths

4. 2 hundred thousands

5. 4 tenths

6. 9 hundred thousands

7. 3 ones

8. 7 tenths

9. 4 thousandths

10. 8 hundredths

11. 4 tens

12. 8 hundred thousands

13. 0 hundredths

14. 4 millions

15. 6 tenths

16. 2 tenths

17. 6 ones

18. 5 hundredths

19. 2 hundredths

20. 9 hundred thousands

21. 8 thousands

22. 0 hundreds

23. 4 hundred thousands

24. 1 ten

25. 7 hundreds

26. 9 hundred thousands

27. 3 hundreds

28. 3 tens

29. 7 thousands

30. 4 tenths

Page 5: Place Value: Expanded Notation

31. 756,818.464

32. 213,045.941

33. 945,749.238

34. 419,165.975

35. 633,670.726

36. 883,217.444

37. 635,507.623

38. 164,536.966

39. 758,327.982

40. 553,725.059   41. 542,832.450   42. 535,566.673

43. 293,340.984   44. 977,975.872   45. 487,494.414

46. 765,363.116   47. 970,920.992   48. 282,629.101

49. 220,481.094   50. 725,588.796   51. 441,579.298

52. 881,327.983   53. 933,645.149   54. 490,598.081

55. 139,662.463   56. 337,984.025   57. 857,500.940

58. 296,116.723   59. 722,280.344   60. 803,756.042

61. 417,465.299   62. 116,495.371

Page 13: Place Value: Expanded Notation

63. 2 hundred thousands + 3 ten thousands + 4 thousands + 2 hundreds + 8 tens + 3 ones + 5 tenths + 4 hundredths + 4 thousandths

64. 3 hundred thousands + 3 thousands + 6 hundreds + 4 tens + 9 ones + 3 tenths + 1 hundredth + 1 thousandth

65. 5 hundred thousands + 9 ten thousands + 8 thousands + 3 hundreds + 6 tens + 3 ones + 5 tenths + 9 hundredths

66. 1 hundred thousand + 4 thousands + 1 hundred + 1 one + 2 tenths + 2 hundredths + 9 thousandths

67. 7 hundred thousands + 4 ten thousands + 9 thousands + 1 hundred + 2 tens + 1 one + 6 tenths + 3 hundredths + 3 thousandths

68. 3 hundred thousands + 3 ten thousands + 8 thousands + 2 hundreds + 6 tens + 7 ones + 5 tenths + 3 thousandths

69. 4 hundred thousands + 9 ten thousands + 5 hundreds + 4 tens + 9 ones + 8 tenths + 3 hundredths + 7 thousandths

70. 4 hundred thousands + 1 ten thousand + 9 hundreds + 9 tens + 9 ones +
3 tenths + 9 hundredths

71. 7 hundred thousands + 6 ten thousands + 8 thousands + 9 hundreds + 1
ten + 9 ones + 1 hundredth + 7 thousandths

72. 3 hundred thousands + 2 ten thousands + 1 thousand + 7 hundreds + 1
ten + 4 ones + 5 tenths + 6 hundredths + 2 thousandths

73. 7 hundred thousands + 6 ten thousands + 2 thousands + 7 hundreds + 1
ten + 1 one + 3 tenths + 7 hundredths + 1 thousandth

74. 2 hundred thousands + 2 ten thousands + 2 thousands + 2 hundreds + 5
tens + 9 ones + 9 tenths + 4 hundredths + 5 thousandths

75. 4 hundred thousands + 8 ten thousands + 7 thousands + 1 hundred + 8
tens + 5 ones + 7 tenths + 7 hundredths + 8 thousandths

76. 4 hundred thousands + 3 ten thousands + 3 thousands + 4 hundreds + 9
tens + 8 tenths + 9 hundredths + 2 thousandths

77. 9 hundred thousands + 8 ten thousands + 9 hundreds + 4 tens + 6 ones +
1 tenth + 8 hundredths

78. 4 hundred thousands + 1 thousand + 4 hundreds + 4 tens + 6 ones + 6
tenths + 9 hundredths + 8 thousandths

79. 7 hundred thousands + 5 ten thousands + 4 thousands + 6 hundreds + 9
tens + 9 ones + 2 tenths + 9 hundredths + 1 thousandth

80. 7 hundred thousands + 3 ten thousands + 9 thousands + 3 hundreds + 8
tens + 8 ones + 8 tenths + 1 thousandth

81. 1 hundred thousand + 4 ten thousands + 4 thousands + 1 hundred + 5
tens + 5 ones + 1 hundredth + 1 thousandth

82. 1 hundred thousand + 7 ten thousands + 9 thousands + 1 hundred + 8 tens + 7 ones + 1 tenth + 8 hundredths + 5 thousandths

83. 3 hundred thousands + 5 ten thousands + 8 thousands + 3 hundreds + 5 tens + 3 ones + 8 hundredths + 2 thousandths

84. 7 hundred thousands + 7 ten thousands + 7 thousands + 8 hundreds + 5 tens + 3 ones + 9 tenths + 3 hundredths + 5 thousandths

85. 1 hundred thousand + 2 ten thousands + 3 thousands + 3 hundreds + 1 one + 1 tenth + 2 hundredths

86. 1 hundred thousand + 5 ten thousands + 3 hundreds + 6 tens + 2 ones + 9 tenths + 6 hundredths + 4 thousandths

87. 3 hundred thousands + 5 ten thousands + 7 hundreds + 2 ones + 2 tenths + 7 hundredths + 7 thousandths

88. 1 hundred thousand + 7 ten thousands + 7 thousands + 3 tens + 5 ones + 7 tenths + 4 hundredths + 6 thousandths

89. 3 hundred thousands + 7 ten thousands + 9 hundreds + 5 tens + 6 ones + 5 hundredths + 5 thousandths

90. 9 hundred thousands + 7 ten thousands + 4 thousands + 1 hundred + 1 ten + 9 ones + 1 tenth + 3 hundredths + 6 thousandths

91. 8 hundred thousands + 6 ten thousands + 1 thousand + 5 hundreds + 8 tens + 9 ones + 9 tenths + 4 hundredths + 8 thousandths

Page 19: Place Value: Expanded Notation

92. 672,085.888	93. 967,311.447	94. 516,430.700
95. 549,409.441	96. 317,842.499	97. 633,222.173
98. 407,932.303	99. 295,852.980	100. 672,424.228
101. 146,398.600	102. 977,813.713	103. 599,034.671

104. 737,849.227   105. 395,785.923   106. 524,566.828

107. 633,207.684   108. 938,350.606   109. 720,356.691

110. 367,940.450   111. 558,437.995   112. 267,279.114

113. 482,173.573   114. 227,680.612   115. 126,713.811

116. 999,947.862   117. 564,855.867   118. 545,711.124

119. 406,908.498   120. 804,607.294

Page 24: Place Value: Expanded Notation

121. 400,000 + 40,000 + 2,000 + 900 + 30 + 2 + 0.5 + 0.02 + 0.007

122. 500,000 + 20,000 + 3,000 + 300 + 90 + 4 + 0.2 + 0.06 + 0.007

123. 400,000 + 30,000 + 4,000 + 200 + 60 + 9 + 0.2 + 0.02 + 0.007

124. 500,000 + 10,000 + 3,000 + 200 + 40 + 7 + 0.3 + 0.03 + 0.007

125. 200,000 + 60,000 + 7,000 + 400 + 20 + 7 + 0.8 + 0.06 + 0.008

126. 800,000 + 80,000 + 9,000 + 700 + 30 + 6 + 0.2 + 0.03 + 0.005

127. 200,000 + 50,000 + 5,000 + 800 + 40 + 4 + 0.3 + 0.05 + 0.009

128. 900,000 + 4,000 + 100 + 40 + 0.9 + 0.06 + 0.007

129. 400,000 + 70,000 + 9,000 + 800 + 7 + 0.2 + 0.05 + 0.001

130. 900,000 + 10,000 + 2,000 + 500 + 5 + 0.1 + 0.02 + 0.009

131. 300,000 + 50,000 + 5,000 + 200 + 90 + 7 + 0.1 + 0.05 + 0.004

132. 600,000 + 90,000 + 6,000 + 800 + 50 + 9 + 0.3 + 0.01 + 0.001

133. 600,000 + 70,000 + 9,000 + 900 + 80 + 3 + 0.9 + 0.05 + 0.008

134. 900,000 + 50,000 + 7,000 + 800 + 20 + 9 + 0.2 + 0.05 + 0.008

135. 700,000 + 90,000 + 2,000 + 200 + 10 + 6 + 0.9 + 0.04 + 0.008

136. 800,000 + 50,000 + 7,000 + 40 + 0.5 + 0.002

137. 900,000 + 30,000 + 3,000 + 600 + 6 + 0.3 + 0.002

138. 300,000 + 10,000 + 7,000 + 800 + 30 + 5 + 0.8 + 0.03 + 0.009

139. 200,000 + 50,000 + 8,000 + 100 + 80 + 3 + 0.7 + 0.002

140. 800,000 + 80,000 + 1,000 + 500 + 90 + 8 + 0.8 + 0.09 + 0.004

141. 100,000 + 20,000 + 5,000 + 800 + 70 + 0.7 + 0.09 + 0.003

142. 300,000 + 90,000 + 1,000 + 700 + 70 + 6 + 0.07 + 0.007

143. 300,000 + 70,000 + 6,000 + 600 + 40 + 0.7 + 0.05 + 0.004

144. 200,000 + 50,000 + 9,000 + 700 + 8 + 0.4 + 0.03

145. 300,000 + 50,000 + 6,000 + 800 + 40 + 3 + 0.4 + 0.03 + 0.002

146. 400,000 + 20,000 + 3,000 + 400 + 7 + 0.9 + 0.09 + 0.004

147. 500,000 + 70,000 + 3,000 + 50 + 6 + 0.3 + 0.08 + 0.003

148. 400,000 + 3,000 + 300 + 20 + 9 + 0.6 + 0.02 + 0.009

149. 200,000 + 5,000 + 700 + 10 + 2 + 0.1 + 0.09 + 0.004

Page 29:   Place Value: Expanded Notation

150. 623,017.674

151. 651,158.346

152. 672,706.335

153. 837,284.274

154. 674,812.324

155. 863,454.667

156. 158,235.874

157. 407,666.865

158. 703,634.726

159. 216,353.783

160. 243,129.723

161. 684,495.860

162. 605,901.007

163. 710,997.219

164. 254,262.962

165. 713,568.542   166. 783,144.786   167. 960,276.406

168. 317,345.188   169. 376,192.581   170. 598,554.840

171. 252,165.091   172. 706,883.749   173. 324,450.624

174. 599,940.120   175. 204,789.061   176. 151,156.450

177. 246,753.513   178. 274,560.797

Page 35: Place Value: Expanded Notation

179. two hundred fifty-six thousand four hundred three and nine hundred five thousandths

180. eight hundred forty-four thousand nineteen and eight hundred seventy-three thousandths

181. four hundred sixteen thousand six hundred seventy-nine and eight hundred fifty-two thousandths

182. eight hundred fifty-two thousand five hundred fourteen and seven hundred twenty-nine thousandths

183. seven hundred ninety-eight thousand four hundred twenty-eight and seven hundred seventy-three thousandths

184. eight hundred fifty-six thousand seven hundred eighty-nine and five hundred seventy-five thousandths

185. three hundred sixty-one thousand three hundred forty-six and seven hundred eighty-three thousandths

186. six hundred eighty-two thousand five hundred ninety and eight hundred eighteen thousandths

187. eight hundred fifty-nine thousand five hundred seventy-five and thirty-six thousandths

188. one hundred five thousand one hundred seventy-one and six hundred thirty-four thousandths

189. one hundred ninety-four thousand three hundred seventy-four and five hundred ninety-one thousandths

190. seven hundred thirty-three thousand nine hundred eighty-one and seventy-four thousandths

191. five hundred forty-nine thousand three hundred seventy-three and six hundred thirty-eight thousandths

192. three hundred twenty-nine thousand nine hundred seventy-one and five hundred seventy-six thousandths

193. two hundred one thousand four hundred eighty-two and fifty-six thousandths

194. one hundred fifteen thousand fifty-three and nine hundred seventy-nine thousandths

195. two hundred ninety-seven thousand one hundred three and thirty-five thousandths

196. five hundred nineteen thousand nine hundred sixty-nine and seven hundred eighty-five thousandths

197. six hundred eighty thousand seven hundred seventy-eight and eight hundred fifty-seven thousandths

198. two hundred twenty-two thousand three hundred seventy-seven and seven hundred ninety-two thousandths

199. five hundred forty-six thousand one hundred thirty-nine and eight hundred eighty-eight thousandths

200. five hundred seventy-three thousand six hundred ninety-eight and six hundred forty-four thousandths

201. four hundred sixty-three thousand one hundred thirty-one and five hundred eighty-seven thousandths

202. three hundred fifty-five thousand seven hundred eleven and one hundred ninety-five thousandth

203. one hundred twenty-seven thousand one hundred thirty-seven and forty-eight thousandths

204. six hundred seven thousand one hundred fifty-seven and three hundred fifty-three thousandths

205. four hundred seventy thousand eight hundred fifty-two and five hundred eighty-three thousandths

206. nine hundred forty-four thousand two hundred seventy-four and five hundred ninety-six thousandths

207. four hundred forty-eight thousand two hundred fifty-five and seven hundred eleven thousandths

208. three hundred thirty-seven thousand three hundred forty-four and one hundred fifty-four thousandth

209. five hundred seventy thousand twenty-three and two hundred sixty-two thousandths

210. eight hundred twelve thousand two hundred ninety-eight and two hundred seventeen thousandths

211. nine hundred eleven thousand four hundred eighty-two and three hundred sixty thousandths

212. two hundred thirty-three thousand one hundred six and sixty-eight thousandths

Page 42:   Rounding Numbers

213. 5,472,000	214. 3,723,340	215. 8,264,499
216. 8,300,000	217. 8,070,000	218. 8,542,076.4
219. 9,000,000	220. 1,310,000	221. 9,235,697.5
222. 9,600,000	223. 2,229,706	224. 6,422,000
225. 1,492,000	226. 9,221,935.2	227. 6,100,000
228. 3,093,970	229. 4,000,000	230. 6,800,000
231. 4,703,775.9	232. 1,240,000	233. 7,284,209
234. 6,827,100	235. 4,809,000	236. 1,609,686.6
237. 8,253,777	238. 2,912,714	239. 5,000,000
240. 4,200,000	241. 3,300,000	242. 6,220,000
243. 5,351,480	244. 3,820,763.7	245. 8,220,000
246. 4,162,675.7	247. 7,827,400	248. 8,291,480
249. 2,886,041	250. 4,650,000	251. 7,120,000
252. 8,266,000	253. 3,300,000	254. 5,152,000
255. 6,501,288.95	256. 5,000,000	257. 2,300,000
258. 4,849,260	259. 5,580,000	260. 5,490,000
261. 4,388,730	262. 2,400,000	263. 9,350,000
264. 8,850,000	265. 4,400,000	266. 8,871,066.4

267. 5,000,000

268. 8,645,255.6

269. 8,910,000

270. 7,654,812.14

271. 1,066,000

272. 6,162,010

273. 4,682,707

274. 5,758,439.93

275. 8,000,000

276. 4,013,390

277. 5,199,600

278. 8,408,942.24

279. 8,200,000

280. 7,329,140

281. 2,390,000

282. 7,762,500

283. 1,207,925.38

284. 9,377,151.8

285. 9,723,217.24

286. 6,438,000

287. 7,900,000

288. 3,133,000

289. 1,325,760

290. 9,730,000

291. 9,282,281

292. 4,000,000

293. 7,333,000

294. 9,372,779.3

295. 9,781,990

296. 2,000,000

297. 6,877,238.14

298. 6,499,000

299. 9,401,557

300. 9,354,000

301. 9,115,824

302. 9,182,150

303. 9,380,000

304. 5,231,229

305. 4,585,184.6

306. 1,962,970

307. 4,583,010

308. 7,500,000

309. 7,190,000

310. 3,490,000

311. 9,880,700

312. 3,900,000

313. 6,652,100

314. 8,250,625

315. 4,092,063.07

316. 7,000,000

317. 2,180,000

318. 9,967,900

319. 9,129,000

320. 7,981,142

321. 1,921,930

322. 2,914,264

323. 8,319,000

324. 9,000,000

325. 8,370,000

326. 6,662,000

327. 8,800,000

328. 5,309,927.25

329. 5,976,000

330. 7,000,000   331. 7,136,151   332. 8,700,000

333. 9,000,000   334. 8,843,207   335. 8,213,312.22

336. 3,212,376   337. 8,390,000   338. 6,000,000

339. 5,791,967.26   340. 8,760,000   341. 2,855,058.1

342. 1,412,964.9   343. 5,900,000   344. 7,840,000

345. 9,847,910.6   346. 6,363,800   347. 7,752,390

348. 9,082,328   349. 6,280,716.2   350. 4,155,800

351. 9,774,095   352. 6,909,300   353. 7,370,621.21

354. 2,000,000   355. 8,431,995   356. 7,201,559.95

357. 1,860,000   358. 1,190,000   359. 6,858,700

360. 7,923,700   361. 3,134,000   362. 9,273,080

363. 2,559,729.1   364. 1,200,000   365. 6,351,700

366. 2,180,000   367. 5,000,000   368. 7,808,920

369. 1,037,313   370. 1,880,000   371. 8,240,683

372. 6,000,000   373. 5,176,000   374. 1,000,000

375. 6,126,084.32   376. 1,508,960   377. 6,966,870

378. 1,000,000   379. 9,340,000   380. 3,008,715

381. 8,909,119   382. 9,746,700   383. 9,000,000

384. 2,820,647.8   385. 7,240,000   386. 1,230,000

387. 2,300,000   388. 8,000,000   389. 1,411,211.7

390. 2,000,000   391. 2,350,000   392. 8,194,326.47

393. 9,118,000   394. 7,868,300

www.ingramcontent.com/pod-product-compliance
Lightning Source LLC
Chambersburg PA
CBHW080942120726
48003CB00011B/3265